MAX FRISCH: Three Plays

MAX FRISCH
Three Plays

Santa Cruz

Now They're Singing Again

Rip van Winkle

TRANSLATED BY
Michael Bullock

INTRODUCTION BY
Peter Loeffler

RONSDALE PRESS

MAX FRISCH: Three Plays
Translation Copyright © 2002 Michael Bullock

All rights reserved. No part of this publication may be reproduced, stored in a retrieval system, or transmitted, in any form or by any means, without prior written permission of the publisher, or, in Canada, in the case of photocopying or other reprographic copying, a licence from CANCOPY (Canadian Copyright Licensing Agency).

Santa Cruz: Copyright 1947 Verlag Benno Schwabe & Co., Klosterberg, Basel. Alle Rechte bei-und vorbehalten durch Suhrkamp Verlag, Frankfurt am Main.
Nun singen sie wieder: Copyright 1946 Verlag Benno Schwabe & Co., Klosterberg, Basel. Alle Rechte bei-und vorbehalten durch Suhrkamp Verlag, Frankfurt am Main.
Rip van Winkle: © 1960 Suhrkamp Verlag, Frankfurt am Main.

RONSDALE PRESS
3350 West 21st Avenue
Vancouver, B.C., Canada
V6S 1G7

Set in Garamond: 11 pt on 15 Adobe Garamond
Typesetting: Julie Cochrane
Printing: AGMV Marquis, Québec
Cover Art: Lori-Anne Latremouille: "Portrait of Max Frisch" (2002) (charcoal & pastel on paper)
Cover Design: Angus Bungay

Ronsdale Press wishes to thank the Canada Council for the Arts, the Department of Heritage, and the British Columbia Cultural Services Branch for their support of its publishing program.

NATIONAL LIBRARY OF CANADA CATALOGUING IN PUBLICATION DATA

Frisch, Max, 1911–1991
    Max Frisch

ISBN 1-55380-000-1

    I. Bullock, Michael, 1918–   II. Title.
PT2611.R814A23 2002   832'.912   C2002-910388-6

*This translation is
dedicated to the memory of
Peter Loeffler, 1938–2002*

CONTENTS

Introduction
9

SANTA CRUZ
27

NOW THEY'RE SINGING AGAIN
117

RIP VAN WINKLE
195

INTRODUCTION

Max Frisch wrote his first play when he was nine years old. His parents, both theatre enthusiasts, had just surprised the boy with a birthday present of a very special kind. In the attic of their house in Zurich they had set up an elaborate toy theatre, complete with a wooden proscenium arch, a pair of painted backdrops, six figurines made of cardboard, and a system of metal tracks to move these figurines in and out of sight.

The young boy was delighted by this present, and indeed in the weeks to come became entranced by it. Manually very dexterous, he supplemented the little toy theatre with further scenic devices. He added the shell of a prompter's box, installed a system of tiny, battery-operated light bulbs, and added a curtain. In short, he persistently began to transform the little stage into a complex miniature world of its own. This perfectly functioning machine, this toy theatre in the attic, however, could only come to life if it was animated by a dramatic event, a scenic impulse, a play. The architectural shell was there; it now had to be imbued with a story.

The nine-year-old Frisch sat down and provided these stories. His first play, a short and grim tale, *The Robber Hotzenplotz,* was barely four pages long; yet, that seemed enough to contain a wedding ceremony, a thunderstorm, the assault on a castle, two songs, a cavalry parade, and a snowstorm. Frisch's dramatic imagination appeared to know no bounds: the little toy theatre had unleashed a world of dramatic fantasies, of fantastic drama.

In years to come this toy theatre was to engage the young boy with unusual force. In a continuous and dynamic process he would re-design and re-construct the little stage, and he would compose scenarios,

INTRODUCTION

sketches, plays to suit his own, his very own theatre. *The Lost Letter (Der verlorene Brief)*, a bloodcurdling melodrama, and *Journey to the Moon (Die Reise auf den Mond)*, a space odyssey patterned on Jules Verne, were particularly successful with the audience of school friends, family, and neighbours that by now gathered every Sunday afternoon for a spectacle in which Frisch was the proud master of ceremonies.

The success of this domestic enterprise led Frisch, in a daring leap of faith, to believe that he was ready for the professional theatre. With the self-confidence, or rather the audacity, that only an adolescent can muster, the fourteen-year-old schoolboy decided to send his newest, most ambitious play, *Steel (Stahl)*, to the German National Theatre. The parcel went off to Berlin. Six weeks of nervous waiting followed, then the answer arrived: it was a politely phrased, yet very firm rejection.

Frisch was devastated. His long-held hopes to succeed in the theatre, hopes that were nourished by his parents and strengthened by his friends, were dashed by one letter. Frisch did not know what to do; and then, suddenly, he did. In a violent romantic, or rather pseudo-romantic gesture, he gathered all of his dramatic scripts, fragments, plans, tied them into two bundles, carried them into the forest of the Zurichberg, and burned them. A chapter was over: his lively little toy theatre suddenly fell into silence.

For years to come Frisch would not write a single dramatic line; the pain inflicted by the letter from Berlin was too acute. But he felt that he had to continue writing. And so, in a very conscious effort to rebuild his self-confidence, he now turned to prose. He began with short, very short stories, his writing still tentative, exploring the miniature form. Soon he became more self-assured. By the time he was nineteen, he had assembled an impressive body of prose writing: short biographical profiles, travel sketches, journals, political essays, short stories, and finally, in 1934, at the age of twenty-four, his first expansive piece of prose, the novel *Jürg Reinhart*. Critics and readers immediately agreed: here was a new voice, both elegant and authentic.

The response to this first novel by an unknown writer was unusual,

INTRODUCTION

both in its force and its degree of sophistication. *Jürg Reinhart* was admired for its narrative economy, its unerring precision in creating multi-layered characters, its clever use of an entire system of ironies, and, above all, for its modernist, self-reflexive stance, that informed the entire text with rich ambiguities.

One of the readers who had been completely taken by Frisch's novel was Kurt Hirschfeld, the Chief Dramaturge of Zurich's Municipal Theatre. He invited the young author to dinner, expressed his enthusiasm, and extended an offer: Frisch should write a play for the Zurich Theatre. The author's response was cautious; he thought he had said farewell to the stage long ago in that incendiary act in the forest. So he resisted. But, over weeks and months, even years, Hirschfeld pursued his offer with diplomacy and force. He twisted Frisch's arm ("almost to the point of breaking his bones", he later recalled), and he finally won. Frisch sat down, after fifteen years of dramatic silence, to write not one play, but two: in a veritable torrent of creativity, within eight weeks, *Santa Cruz* and *Now They're Singing Again* were born. A spell had been broken; Frisch was a playwright once again.

The young author, who was thirty-three by now, could not have been offered a more stimulating venue for his enterprise. The Municipal Theatre of Zurich was, quite simply, the strongest company in Switzerland. It could boast a small, yet splendidly equipped stage; it had over decades managed to attract a uniquely ambitious and gifted group of actors, directors and designers; and it could rely on an audience that was young, intellectually curious, and very demanding.

The crucial year of 1933 had brought with it another substantial strengthening of the company. Hitler's access to power had driven many of the leading theatre artists out of Germany. A considerable group of these refugees found a safe haven in Zurich, and within weeks they were integrated into an already stellar company. By the time Max Frisch began his collaboration with the Zurich Theatre, it fully deserved its title as the most prestigious theatre company not only in Switzerland, but in all of the German-speaking world.

INTRODUCTION

Kurt Hirschfeld, who over a lifetime was to become Frisch's closest friend, his most generous mentor, and his severest, sincerest critic, was the intellectual force of this theatre. His uncompromising anti-fascist stance and his rigorous aesthetic standards shaped what theatre historians have come to call "The Zurich Dramaturgy". The heart of this dramaturgical program was the systematic fostering of new talent. Hirschfeld was convinced that the true dramatist did not write *for* the stage, but *with* the stage. He therefore actively encouraged the integration of prospective stage writers into the day-to-day process of theatre-making. Frisch, too, was invited to this inclusive method of working and learning: he attended rehearsals of all the plays in the repertory; he sat in on discussions with the design team; took actors aside to argue over subtle shadings in the script; deliberated with technicians on lighting cues; discussed any use of incidental music. In short, Frisch was intimately familiarized with the craft of staging. He came to realize that the dramatist was more than simply a provider of words, but had to become the creator of a rich *theatrical* emblem. This was the lesson Frisch learned under the mentorship of Kurt Hirschfeld. It was a lesson that was put to a test, and to splendid success, in his first full-length play, *Santa Cruz*.

* * *

Santa Cruz tells the story of a stern, hard-edged army captain who uses all of the instruments of patriarchy with unbending force. He seems to enjoy limitless wealth, and resides in a castle that is lavishly maintained by a varied set of servants whom he bellows at and orders around as if he were on the battlefield. For seventeen years now he has been married to Elvira, a woman of ethereal beauty and a delicate mind; but the marriage has turned into an emotional wasteland. One night, in the midst of winter, a poor, handsome, mysterious stranger begs to be let into the castle, where he is fed by the servants, given new clothes, and a bundle of hay to sleep on. Next morning, it is a Sunday, he is introduced to the castle's master and mistress, who each respond to the intruder in very

INTRODUCTION

different ways. The Captain is suspicious and immediately senses a threat to his dominant control. Elvira, however, quite helplessly and hopelessly falls under the intoxicating spell of the stranger. Who is he? Could he be that mysterious sailor with whom, seventeen years ago, she spent one single rapturous night? Is he the liberator she has so fervently been dreaming of, who could free her from the wasteland of her marriage? Could he, by some magic coincidence, be the father of her child, who has just turned seventeen? Or was he, beyond all romantic linkages, simply a good-looking beggar asking for food and shelter on a snowy winter night? Elvira does not know, and will never know, for the stranger dies of a mysterious affliction. His seven-day visit to the castle has set forth a range of turbulences, of hopes, fears, memories and desires, but, in the end, has not effected any change. The marriage continues, locked into what seems an eternal stalemate, until, some day, some night, another stranger might knock at the door . . .

Frisch's first play was a fairy tale. The term he himself used was "romance" *(Romanze)*, and indeed *Santa Cruz* is a poetic meditation on *Sehnsucht*, that eternally unfulfilled yearning for something beyond the coarseness of the material world. This yearning for complete transcendence beyond the deadening codes of rule and order propels Elvira. Touched, or rather burned, by the liberating grace of the stranger, she dreams of shedding the chains of bondage. What she so fervently longs for is the revolutionary act of being, instead of simply seeming. This desperate attempt to celebrate one's authentic self, this longing for a holy communion beyond the law of domestic convention, places Elvira securely in the late-romantic tradition of heroines with eternally unfulfilled desires.

In conversations about *Santa Cruz* Frisch has repeatedly referred to his first play as a seasonal battle *(ein Kampf der Jahreszeiten)*. In this conceptual model the Captain represents the figure of Winter, enthroned in his castle, which is covered, like a shroud, by thick layers of snow. The wells are frozen, the bitter cold seeps indoors, and forces everyone to be packed in fur and thick cloth. It is the world of the

INTRODUCTION

frozen heart. The castle has turned into an ice palace, ruled by the King of Winter.

But there is the other world, the world of adventure, of passion, of pleasure and heat. It is the world of the stranger, who comes not from the frozen north, but from the steaming, tropical seas of the south. He is turbulence, fertility, intoxication, danger, and life. He is the dynamic principle, always in motion, always in commotion. He is, with his laurel of vines, the God of Spring.

Elvira stands on the battlefield of these formidable forces, torn by the reality of winter and the promise of spring. The tensions of duty and pleasure, of rule and freedom, and, ultimately, of Thanatos and Eros, come to shape her life, a life that ends in darkness, with Elvira submitting to the yoke of a loveless marriage once again.

Lebendig begraben, buried alive, was an earlier title of this play. It is a hard and bitter play, with Winter in command. And yet, at the very end, literally in the last few lines, there is hope, or at least the faint glimmer of hope. The daughter appears, very real and tangible, and yet almost like an apparition, to offer, however faintly, a new beginning. As long as we believe in adventure, Frisch seems to imply, and as long as we continue to hope, there will be renewal, and spring will, possibly, return.

In *Santa Cruz* Frisch deals with a grand topic in a bold and adventurous manner, and stylistically, too, he takes some extraordinary risks. One of the more striking dramatic features is Frisch's highly inventive and complex handling of time. Instead of relying on the proven dramatic formula of chronometric progression, Frisch constructs a temporal frame in which various time-levels overlap and interlock. What he achieves in the process is a conglomeration of time, in which the past is very tangibly brought in through re-enactment, and where the future is forcefully evoked in verbal fantasies. Seventeen years of marriage and seven days of the stranger's visit collapse into the real time of theatrical performance. What we, as readers and audience, witness is the contraction of measured and imagined time into one single, immensely rich and complex temporal experience. Ever fond of geological imagery,

INTRODUCTION

Frisch has compared this to the violent shifting of tectonic plates, where, in the process of commotion, the layers have begun and continue to interpenetrate in the most surprising ways. Time, Frisch argued, cannot be captured in any linear, mechanistic model; it defies chronometry, and must be understood as something he once called "continuous undulation" *(ewige Wellenbewegung)*.

According to Frisch, not only our temporal experience, but our spatial sense, too, is informed by this undulation. In *Santa Cruz* the scenes shift, slide and slither continuously from one dramatic locale to the other. They do this with dream-like assurance, and with no need to justify their shift in any rational, reasonable way. The castle's kitchen; the deck of the pirate ship on the high seas; the seedy brothel near the harbour; the ominous chamber of death: all these locales are sketched out by Frisch with the loving care of the realist. And yet, in their collective summation they all add up to a richly patterned *mythic* space that embraces a variety of worlds in one potent and complete scenic metaphor.

Frisch's deliberate and artful play with time and space brings *Santa Cruz* as a dramatic construct very close to the experience of a dream. In both there is the fluidity of time that seems to move, then halt, and then move again at ever shifting speed, and in ever changing directions; and in both our sense of space is always surprisingly located, then re-located and dis-located, in a torrent of prismatic images. Linearity of plot and clarity of action are abandoned, to give way to a dramatic narrative that replicates the particular and peculiar laws of the dream.

But whose dream is being dreamt? Is it the Captain's fantasy of power, or is it Elvira's dream of liberation? Is it the servants' proletarian dream of freedom, or the daughter's dream of a returning spring? Or could it be Max Frisch's collective dream, that subsumes all the dreams of all the characters? Like any good artist, Frisch provides us with questions, but refuses an answer. What he leaves us with in *Santa Cruz* is a dramatic metaphor of infinite complexity, that is as rich and rewarding, but ultimately as impenetrable as a dream.

INTRODUCTION

* * *

Max Frisch conceived, wrote, and revised the first two plays of this volume concurrently, within a couple of months in early 1944, and, not surprisingly, they share some similarities, both in theme and in style. And yet they differ in one striking way. While *Santa Cruz* was framed as a dramatic fairy tale that lifted us out of time into a mythic dimension, *Now They're Singing Again* was rooted in the immediacy of a raging war.

The date of composition is crucial. As military historians tell us, 1944 was to become the most horrifying year of a horrifying war. The German army, sensing that the balance of success was no longer tipping in its favour, resorted to a strategy of burnt earth *(verbrannte Erde)*. In a dangerous mix of despair and ferocity, total war was declared. Acts of destruction now reached far beyond the battleground. In ever increasing numbers civilians were caught and destroyed by the now all-encompassing war machine. Mass executions of enemies, or perceived traitors within their own ranks, became daily, hourly occurrences. Hamlets, villages, towns, cities, were by now, indiscriminately, open to attack. Central Europe, Germany above all, had turned into a slaughterhouse; it was now, in early 1944, indeed a total war.

When Frisch wrote *Now They're Singing Again (Nun singen sie wieder)*, Switzerland was living through the most precarious period of its history. The tiny country was now surrounded on all four sides by the enemy, so that there were no geographic links to any of the Allied forces left. The Germans fully realized the strategic importance of this country; detailed invasion plans were prepared, and the German army was ready to strike at any moment.

Switzerland, however, was fiercely committed to strike back. All through the war years it had trained a disproportionately small army that was willing to throw itself into the defence of its country. Frisch, like all young men of his age, had been conscripted into this small army. Photographs from the period show him in uniform, invariably with a notebook, the writer's pad, in his hand. In these notebooks *Now*

INTRODUCTION

They're Singing Again was born. The play had grown, very directly, from the world of war.

In *Now They're Singing Again* Frisch constructs a plotline of deceiving simplicity. It presents us with the story of Karl, a young, mature, sensitive German soldier, who is forced, single-handedly, to execute twenty-one hostages. Under the threat of death, with a gun at his forehead, he complies, but remains deeply traumatized by the experience. When he is ordered, in a further step, to kill any possible witness, he cracks under the pressure of shame, deserts the army, roams the battle-torn country shaken by guilt, and is eventually touched by madness. Seeing no way out of his torturous existence, he kills himself.

Frisch presents the story line as simple, yet the ethical implications as exceedingly complex. The play asks a whole set of questions that philosophers have tried to answer over the course of history: Why do people kill? Why did Cain raise his club against Abel? Why do we blindly, slavishly follow orders? Why can we so easily be seduced into criminal complicity? How can we live with the weight of our daily betrayals? What is guilt? Is forgiveness possible? Does God care?

Frisch raises, sometimes merely evokes, these questions, but he adamantly refuses any clear-cut answer. He never mistakes the stage for a pulpit from which to sermonize; nor is he the ideologue, standing on a soapbox and dispensing facile, quickly applicable solutions. These questions defy easy answers; perhaps, Frisch argues, they defy any answer at all. This world, particularly in the turbulent context of war, becomes an experience riddled with internal contradictions; now even the simplest questions can turn into hieroglyphs. Who is the victim? Who is the perpetrator? Frisch implies, or at least seems to imply, that once the murderous energies of a war are unleashed at full force, the lines between the opposing groups begin to blur, as we are *all* engaged in a massive, ultimately senseless act of destruction.

And so *Now They're Singing Again* does not take sides *against* the Germans or *for* the Allies, but it very quietly and humbly aligns itself with the improbable, perhaps even impossible, mission for peace. In

INTRODUCTION

this sense Frisch's second play distinctly stands in the long tradition of pacifist drama, ranging from Aeschylus through Schiller to Brecht.

When Frisch sat down to compose the first draft of *Now They're Singing Again,* he still thought that he could present the story within a realistic frame, as a faithful document of a very real war. He soon rejected this approach, though, as he came to realize that the immensity of the horror he was dealing with could only be captured on stage within an expressive, expressionist mode. What he now aimed for, in his second, third, and then final draft, was the style of a heightened fable, close in tone to *Santa Cruz.* But while *Santa Cruz* had chosen the hidden logic of a dream as its dramaturgical principle, *Now They're Singing Again* was patterned on the far more disruptive, jagged dynamics of a nightmare.

Frisch presents us with a world consumed by fire; it is not the cleansing fire of purgatory, however, but the eternally torturing fire of hell. A truly Dantesque vision arises with horrible force: children are being torn from their mothers' arms and tossed into boiling tar; judges without name and face hastily sign a stack of death warrants; a bomber squadron, heavily drugged on cheap liquor, revels in the obliteration of two cities; while the flames of the fire, and the flames of hatred, creep into every house, into every heart.

And yet, despite the seeming dissolution of all ethical values, despite the hellish destruction of all beauty, despite the imminent apocalypse, there is hope, or at least a glimmer of hope. In *Santa Cruz* the apparition of the young girl at the very end signals the possibility of a new beginning. Here, in *Now They're Singing Again,* it is the Song of the Dead that offers solace and hope. Frisch's sense of dramatic irony is potent and complete. While the living are blinded by hate, and enmeshed in a maze of guilt, it is only the dead that can see and claim innocence. They are the truly free: free from hate, free from ambition, free from the gravity of this earth. And so, as they intone their song, they present us, the living and the lost, with a humble and intense requiem, with a simple plea for peace.

INTRODUCTION

* * *

Santa Cruz and *Now They're Singing Again* were both given their world premiere at the Zurich Theatre in the season of 1944/45. Kurt Hirschfeld, who by now had become Frisch's paternal mentor in all matters related to drama and staging, made sure that all conditions of performance were as conducive as possible. Realizing the complexity of these plays, he insisted, for example, on a rehearsal period that was clearly longer than the one conceded by the unions. In close consultation with the author, issues about casting were discussed. Decisions were not always easy to make, as the stellar troupe of players offered multiple choices, all of them convincing.

Hirschfeld's patient role as dramaturgical advisor and his active concern for all aspects of production handsomely paid off in the end. Both plays were warmly, indeed enthusiastically, received by the audience, an audience that was eager to hear a fresh voice, even if this voice expressed itself in a complex tone. These plays were not easily accessible; they demanded and deserved an audience that could be, at the same time, patient and adventurous. The Zurich audience of *Santa Cruz* and *Now They're Singing Again* was just that: young, responsive, and intellectually alert. Its unwavering support for these two plays set the foundation-stone for Frisch's eventual career as the best-known dramatist of his generation writing in German.

Frisch's success as a writer, particularly in a medium as public as the theatre, rewarded him threefold: it gave him visibility with the audience, respect from the critics, and it eventually provided him with a measure of wealth. Financially independent, Frisch could now indulge in one of his true passions, travelling. From short, cursory sidetrips to extended sabbatical leaves, Frisch would explore and expand his vision of the world in the act of travelling. On one of these longer sojourns, in the United States, he was to come across the raw material that, eventually, fed into the third text of this volume, *Rip van Winkle*.

At a reception after a reading at Boston University in 1951, Frisch was approached by a graduate student who told him, in rough outlines,

INTRODUCTION

the story of Rip van Winkle; it was a story Frisch had vaguely heard of before, but never had the time to pursue any further. The re-telling of this American fable by an excited student immediately aroused Frisch's interest. Next morning he headed to a bookstore, and picked up a heavily worn, but magnificently illustrated, second-hand copy of *Rip van Winkle,* in a version re-told for children. This was the beginning of a long literary journey, for the story of Rip eventually made its way into Frisch's work in a perplexing multitude of ways. It first filtered into his journals, then into the sketch of a play, then it metamorphosed, in a further step, into an unfinished filmscript, and finally, into its present form, as a dramatic narrative for radio.

The bare outline of the story is simple. Plagued by the narrowness of domestic life, Rip van Winkle takes to the open road, ventures into unknown territory, where he meets a band of dwarfs, who invite him to a game of ninepins and a drink from a small, suspiciously heavy keg. Rip accepts the offer, plays ninepins, drinks from the mysterious keg, and falls into a deep sleep. When he awakens, the dwarfs are gone, and Rip, to his amazement, has turned into an old man with leathery skin and a long white beard: he had been sleeping for forty years. Confused and frightened he returns to his village, where no one recognizes him any longer. For the rest of his life he will now have to live as a stranger among his own people.

Frisch was intrigued by this story, particularly by its simplicity that reminded him of a woodcut. What truly struck him, however, was the dimension that lingered beneath the surface of the simple folk-tale. Frisch very soon came to see how the central issue of this fable related to one of the grand themes of Western philosophy, namely the quest for authentic selfhood. It was a theme that spanned all the way from Aristotle over Descartes to the ontologists of his own day, and that Pirandello, the playwright closest to Frisch's heart, had made the centre of his dramatic universe. Like Pirandello, whose characters are in search of an author, Frisch, too, asks the ever elusive, ever evasive, question

INTRODUCTION

about the self of selfhood. When, in the flux of time, are we truly ourselves? If change is at the core of all living, can there be any such thing as the stability of self? Who, really, is Rip van Winkle? Are we who we think we are, or are we defined, and entrapped, by the gaze of others? Every tentative answer leads to another question, and further complicates the philosophical puzzle: who are we in this maze of mirrors?

Frisch was intrigued by these concerns because they were linked in a direct and painful way to his own biographical experience: they reflect, in an ironic mirror, his tense, even troubled relation with his own country. He, too, like Rip, had gone abroad, had been on many journeys, both literal and metaphorical, he had changed, had acquired another, a richer self, had returned home, only to find that the country he had left behind did not comprehend, let alone accept, his change, simply because he now no longer passively fitted the mould. And so, beyond two cultures and two continents, Frisch felt a clear affinity to the American folk figure. He, too, had become a stranger at home. "Rip van Frisch" he noted with bitter irony on the margin of his manuscript.

And yet, despite this bitter personal link, Frisch decided to deal with these issues of philosophy and biography in a distinctly comic vein. While *Santa Cruz* and *Now They're Singing Again* were conceived as profoundly grim stories that precluded any form of humour, Frisch now relied on the entire arsenal of comic techniques to make his point. It is as if he wanted to explore territory that he had so far only tentatively entered. And so subtle touches of irony are just as effectively used as the bold strokes of satire, while the play of words ranges from subtle innuendo to overt punning. His true mastery, however, shows itself in his use of caricature. Frisch very deliberately pushes his figures — the lawyer, the doctor, the wife — far into the realm of distortion, without, though, ever losing their firm anchor in a real and recognizable world. Like any true caricaturist, Frisch knows exactly where to stop, in order to make the caricature as real, funny, and biting as possible. *Rip van Winkle* is high philosophy and low comedy; that it is both in such a

INTRODUCTION

unified blend confirms Frisch's full grasp of the comic form. The Philosopher as Clown: in Frisch's *Rip van Winkle* this difficult doubling is fully achieved.

* * *

Why should we read, and re-read, these early plays? What do they tell us about themselves? And what do they tell us about us? Many reasons could be mentioned; three seem of particular note. First: the early texts presented in this volume are all intriguing prefigurations of Frisch's later, better known work. In seed form, and often more, all the grand themes that he was to wrestle with throughout his life are already present, sometimes overtly, sometimes in a more subliminal link. The theme of an unlived, unloved life, for example, that constitutes the core of *Santa Cruz*, blossoms more than two decades later into one of Frisch's masterpieces, *Biography*. The question of how we can maintain our integrity amidst the hellfires of war is addressed with equal force in the early *Now They're Singing Again* and in the later *The War is Over*. And *Rip van Winkle*'s questioning of identity, that culminates in the acceptance of a new self, foreshadows the theme of wilful image-making that is at the centre of Frisch's greatest prose achievement, *Stiller*.

Frisch is a metamorphic writer, continuously changing shape, crossing the border from essay to novel, from drama to journal to sketch and pamphlet with astonishing ease. To discover the firm constants, the thematic anchors, within these perplexing transmutations of Frisch's long career, is a difficult, intriguing task. In this task a reading of the early, formative plays can assist us.

A second reason for reading these plays: the early texts provide us with an extraordinarily sensuous feast, in which the author draws from all dramatic conventions known to him. Frisch had always been a voracious reader who seemed to have no inhibitions in absorbing any of the lessons he learned into his writing, as long as they served his narrative purpose. This assimilation was so authentic and complete that the sin-

INTRODUCTION

gle stones taken from other traditions often fully integrate, and thus disappear, in Frisch's new mosaic.

A patient reading, however, will reveal the immense and carefully wrought complexity of this mosaic. And so we hear echoes of Greek tragedy, of medieval allegory, and the baroque dream play in the tradition of Calderon; we find elements of the fairy tale and of the ballad, the Jesuit debate and vaudeville, parable and slapstick, expressionist fantasy and the remnants of the well-made play: from these, and many more, seemingly disparate elements Frisch forges a new dramatic entity of kaleidoscopic wealth.

"All art is collaboration": J.M. Synge's admirably inclusive line fits perfectly to describe Max Frisch's poetic world. By reading him, and his early plays, we are gently invited into a dialogue with an entire canonic tradition. All drama, right down to Frisch's own time, resonates in his work with convincing force.

The third point that explains the appeal of these early plays is straightforward and direct: Frisch convincingly proves to have a complete, unwavering instinct for the laws of theatre. The three plays presented here satisfy us as poetry, politics, and philosophy, but it is as perfect vehicles for the living stage that they exert their greatest force. The way, for example, Frisch sets up a scenic unit by carefully establishing, and then raising, lowering, continuously manipulating its inherent dramatic charge, is, quite simply, masterful. It is as masterful as the creation of the entire gallery of richly individualized characters and sharply drawn caricatures that have attracted, for good and obvious reasons, the best actors of their generation.

Max Frisch's plays are difficult to stage. In strictly technical terms they do not offer any problems; they can be, and indeed very successfully have been, performed in simple black-box theatres, with only the slightest indication of scenery. So while their technical challenges are minimal, the intrinsic structure of the plays requires a director of a very special and rare kind. With each of his plays Frisch creates an infinite-

INTRODUCTION

ly complex, polyphonic organism, with carefully built-in dramatic weights and counterweights. Directors who are rushed for time, or are simply lazy, too often disregard this complexity in favour of a reductionist, monophonic voice. This voice might be cleaner and clearer, but it does harmful disservice to the perplexing, bewildering ambiguity that sits at the centre of each of Frisch's dramatic parables.

Any translator of Frisch's work faces a very similar set of challenges, for the language of these plays encompasses an astonishing range: it reaches from casual, colloquial, even chatty speech, often tinged with touches of dialect, to the metaphorically charged, densely woven language of poetry. Then there is Frisch's sharply observant use of language as a social classifier: the jargon of the military, with each rank carefully identified by its linguistic profile, is as convincingly captured as the lawyer's legalese, while the policeman, in turn, speaks differently from any member of the clergy. In these plays it becomes wonderfully clear, and miraculously audible, that characters are not only defined by what they say, but by how they say it.

A further challenge for the translator is what Frisch has called the "temperature" of language. It could reach from the icy coldness of a snap military order to a heated sigh of longing, with unnameable tonal gradations in between. As a lover of music, Frisch was fully aware that language, and most conspicuously spoken language, was propelled not only by its tonality, but by an inherent rhythmic impulse. Carefully set up accelerations, and equally meticulous retardations, could convey, with seismographic precision, the state of the speaker, the mood of a scene, the tone of an entire passage. Writing thus meant orchestrating, giving each voice the clarity and expressiveness of an instrument. *Sprache muss atmen*, language has to breathe, was one of Frisch's favourite comments on the craft of writing. His plays, with their rich and magnificently precise language, do full justice to this poetologic demand.

To find the right translator is all too often a matter of good luck. Frisch could not have been luckier in finding Michael Bullock, his translator into English. Bullock combines an absolute idiomatic assured-

INTRODUCTION

ness with a keen ear for every rhythmic cadence. He is unwilling to sacrifice precision for a choice that might sound clever but betrays the original. Bullock serves the primary text both as a poet and a scholar: the encyclopaedic richness of Frisch is captured in its freewheeling spirit and in its meticulously codified letter. And above all: Bullock provides a translation that does not sound like one. The new text is more than a shadow: it very assuredly rests in itself, carries its very own intrinsic weight. André Gide, who has so profoundly and perceptively speculated on the art of translation, has said that its ultimate test is whether "it sings" (" . . . que ça chante"). Bullock's translation of Max Frisch passes and surpasses this test; with its high craft and elegant ease it simply, and very enchantingly, "sings".

— Peter Loeffler, Professor of Theatre
University of British Columbia
August 2001

SANTA CRUZ
A Romance

CHARACTERS:

Elvira, a fifty-three-year-old woman • Viola, her daughter
• The Cavalry Captain, her husband • Pelegrin, a vagabond •
A Landlady • A Doctor • A Servant • A Secretary • A Lad
• A Negro • A Policeman • Pedro, a poet in irons •
Tenant Farmers • Sailors • Lookout • Gravediggers
• A Man • Ten Ghostly Figures

The play takes place in seven days
and in seventeen years.

PRELUDE

In an inn. In the background sit tenant farmers halfheartedly playing cards. In the foreground are the doctor and the vagabond, who is sitting on the table playing a guitar and humming. Wind is blowing outside.

VAGABOND: A Javanese song, Doctor; that's what the sailors, those brown devils with cat's eyes, always used to sing when we lay up on the quarterdeck and couldn't sleep for the heat! We sailed round the Cape, we sailed for seven weeks on end, our barrels stank to high heaven, but the moon hung like a silver gong over the sea, it hung like a Chinese lantern between our masts . . . and they sang this song over and over again, all night long, all those nights without wind.

(He hums it again)

DOCTOR: *(Calling)* Josephine?

(A man has entered and shakes down his coat)

A MAN: Ugh, what a snowstorm! They're having another burial over in the churchyard, Doctor. When they came along singing hymns and burning incense, with the corpse in front, I'm damned if they could find the grave —

(Moving away)

that's how hard it's snowing out there.

(He sits down)

I'll have a brandy.

DOCTOR: We'll have another bottle over here, Josephine.

(Landlady leaves)

VAGABOND: She loved me.

DOCTOR: Who?

VAGABOND: Maybe I behaved like a scoundrel, seventeen years ago, and yet, believe me, Doctor, she loved me — she loved me the way people believe in a miracle, without reservations!

DOCTOR: Who?

VAGABOND: I couldn't think of any other way of seeing her again; I needed a ship, any ship I could get hold of — we seized her as she lay off the coast of Morocco. The poor Frenchies! We chucked them overboard, drunk as they were, splash, splash, splash! We painted over the coat of arms. We hoisted the sail, and for thirteen weeks I sailed after her.

DOCTOR: Who?

VAGABOND: I can't help laughing when I think of her father! I have a pearl of a daughter, he said, but you, lads, aren't good enough even to look at her. Where is she then? I asked. That's none of your business, growled the old gentleman: she's engaged.

DOCTOR: Engaged?

VAGABOND: To a nobleman, to a cavalry captain!

DOCTOR: Seriously?

VAGABOND: Seriously: that same night she was on my ship, in my arms, in my cabin —

DOCTOR: Who?

VAGABOND: Elvira, a magnificent girl.

DOCTOR: Elvira? Our Cavalry Captain's wife? The mistress up at our castle?

VAGABOND: Hush!

(Landlady brings a fresh bottle)

LANDLADY: Gentlemen, this is my last bottle.

DOCTOR: Our friend is thirsty.

LANDLADY: So it seems.

DOCTOR: Our friend has been around the world, you know; he has been through more than a Josephine can dream of —

LANDLADY: How do you know what I can dream of?

DOCTOR: He went around the world, I say, until the fever got him.

LANDLADY: The fever?

DOCTOR: For a whole year he hasn't been allowed to drink anything, you know. Now we're celebrating his recovery!

LANDLADY: Congratulations . . .

(She fills the glasses)

If it's true.

VAGABOND: It's true all right!

LANDLADY: Let's hope so, sir. The good doctor is always telling people they're well; he likes people, that's why he tells so many lies.

VAGABOND: Don't worry, woman, he didn't tell me any lies, not one word.

LANDLADY: How do you know?

VAGABOND: How do I know? Because he didn't say a word; I had to tell him myself that I was well!

LANDLADY: Oh, in that case . . .

VAGABOND: Better than I've ever been in my life.

LANDLADY: Good luck to you.

(She sits down with them)

LANDLADY: Sometimes it has worked out differently, you know. We've seen people drinking and laughing and celebrating their recovery, and a month later the man was lying in the churchyard over there, the one who had recovered. In fact it's always like that . . . Well, I'm just telling you how it was . . . And he does all that out of pure humanity, you know; he works away curing people till there's no hope; and then his kind heart takes over. Why shouldn't they have fun, he says, the people for whom there's no hope?

VAGABOND: Don't worry, good woman —

LANDLADY: I know, I know!

VAGABOND: In a month you say?

LANDLADY: Holy Mary, don't get me wrong! . . .

(He laughs)

VAGABOND: In a month, good woman, I shall be way out at sea again!

(He drinks)

Seriously, my dear Doctor, there's a farm waiting for me in Cuba, abandoned, burnt down and dried up — a farm that will produce fruit: pineapples, peaches, plums, figs, grapes! The ship sails in a month. In one year, I give you my word, you will get the first lot of coffee.

LANDLADY: Coffee?

VAGABOND: All those weeks when I was lying up there, sick and hopeless, damned in a hell of fever, a prisoner in your hospital, and everyone who said an encouraging word to me felt embarrassed, because he thought he was lying when he said that I should get better, that I should stand on these legs again, go where I felt like going. During all those weeks that are over and done with, I kept thinking to myself: Oh, to drink a bottle again, to be among living people again.

DOCTOR: I know, you often used to say that.

VAGABOND: And now?

DOCTOR: The bottle isn't empty yet —

VAGABOND: Just look at these people!

DOCTOR: I can see them.

VAGABOND: Why don't they live?

DOCTOR: How do you mean?

VAGABOND: Who are they?

DOCTOR: Tenant farmers.

VAGABOND: Life is short. Don't you know that? Why don't they sing? Why don't they live? . . . Live —

(Noise among the farmers)

FIRST: Lick my ass.

SECOND: I'll bring the oxen over tomorrow —

FIRST: I won't feed them, I told you that two days ago at the market, even if the devil himself comes with them, I won't feed them —

THIRD: In the spring, when we can hitch them to the plough, you'll be glad to have them.

FIRST: In the spring!

THIRD: The Cavalry Captain meant well —

FIRST: Meant well! Anyone can buy oxen, if he has money. And if his tenant has to feed them! Next week is Martinmas, and I'll tell our Cavalry Captain straight out, to his face: Meaning well and doing well, Your Honour, are two different things.

THIRD: Talk like that will spoil everything . . .

FIRST: Trump!

(They continue playing, but now they slap the cards on the table)

VAGABOND: Who are those fellows?

LANDLADY: Tenant farmers.

DOCTOR: They belong to the castle.

VAGABOND: To the castle?

DOCTOR: As the horse belongs to the cart.

LANDLADY: For months they've been arguing every evening about the two oxen the Captain bought for them: the best thing would be to ask the oxen what's to be done with them.

VAGABOND: The Captain, you said?

LANDLADY: Our Cavalry Captain! As the people round here say. Our castle! And yet not one of them has ever been inside the castle since the day he was born.

VAGABOND: Why not?

LANDLADY: They don't let anyone in. Apart from the tenants, of course, when they bring their goose at Martinmas.

VAGABOND: Why don't they let anyone in?

LANDLADY: Why not? Go and ask, if you want to know; just try, the Captain will be delighted to meet you!

VAGABOND: Why?

LANDLADY: A man of order, a man like him, the exact opposite of a vagabond . . .

VAGABOND: What does he look like?

LANDLADY: The Captain?

VAGABOND: Well — shall we say: Like an eagle who smokes a pipe?

DOCTOR: Exactly like that!

LANDLADY: Like an eagle who smokes a pipe —

VAGABOND: And has he got children too?

DOCTOR: A little daughter.

VAGABOND: Ah —

DOCTOR: Does that surprise you?

VAGABOND: A little daughter . . .

LANDLADY: There are all sorts of rumours, if you want to know. People say she doesn't look a bit like her father, the sweet child . . . I'm just telling you what people say; heavens above, a cavalry captain's wife is also a woman, a cavalry captain's wife was also young once.

VAGABOND: Isn't she young any longer? . . .

LANDLADY: He says that as if he really felt sorry! She's been around in the world too, I can tell you —

VAGABOND: May I ask you another question?

LANDLADY: What is it?

VAGABOND: What is her name?

LANDLADY: Whose?

VAGABOND: The mother's, the Cavalry Captain's wife, the mistress of the castle.

LANDLADY: Why do you want to know?

VAGABOND: . . . Elvira?

LANDLADY: It seems to me, my good sir, that you already know all about it.

VAGABOND: Oh . . . not really —

(He plucks his guitar)

A beautiful name for a beautiful dame.

(The clatter of shoes is heard)

LANDLADY: Heavens above, who can that be?

(Landlady goes out)

DOCTOR: You seem taken aback, my friend.

VAGABOND: I'm going to the castle.

DOCTOR: You? You mean that seriously?

VAGABOND: I'm going to the castle.

DOCTOR: Do you think they will let you in?

VAGABOND: To be among living people again . . . You mean because of my shoes, because of my jacket? She loved me. Just as I am. Why shouldn't we say hello to one another? . . . That's all I want . . . We shall be alone together for a little while, Elvira and I. I shall hold the candle. I shan't kiss her. We won't profane the past. We won't repeat anything. I shall see her breathing. That will be enough for me. And tomorrow I shall move on.

DOCTOR: That's how it will be, exactly like that!

VAGABOND: However it may be, Doctor, it will be life, life once again —

(Two men enter and lean their spades against the wall)

LANDLADY: Hey, where is he off to? What's the idea? Hey, where are you off to with the guitar? . . . Eh? . . . Vagabond! . . .

(The landlady runs after him)

SHORT GRAVEDIGGER: I must say, Doctor, you give us gravediggers a lot of work with your cures up there. Work means earnings, I always say, and honest earnings, I always say, because we work for our money, a whole cold morning, and people have to die anyway. So why shouldn't they come here to do it — we live by it, I say to myself . . .

(The Landlady returns)

A MAN: Well, gravediggers, did you find it?

TALL GRAVEDIGGER: Did we find what?

A MAN: I mean the grave.

SHORT GRAVEDIGGER: Damn it all, we dug and shovelled a fathom deep this morning, you couldn't dig a better grave than that; since I received the blessing, I've dug around seventy graves —

TALL GRAVEDIGGER: Did they ever find the grave?

SHORT GRAVEDIGGER: The parson found it.

A MAN: How come?

TALL GRAVEDIGGER: Very simple, friend, very simple —

SHORT GRAVEDIGGER: All of a sudden, prayerbook in hand, he sank in the snow — whoosh — down he went, along with his words of comfort.

TALL GRAVEDIGGER: So now we'll have a brandy, a good strong brandy.

(The farmers, who have been listening over their cards, pass comments on the story)

FIRST FARMER: Who?

SECOND FARMER: The parson!

(The farmers laugh)

LANDLADY: The rogue, running off with my guitar like that . . . and the snow so deep . . . It's all very well for you to laugh, it's my guitar, not your guitar!

DOCTOR: I'm not laughing.

LANDLADY: Running off like that!

DOCTOR: Don't worry, Josephine. You'll get your guitar back.

LANDLADY: That's what you say —

DOCTOR: I guarantee it.

LANDLADY: When? When?

DOCTOR: Very soon.

LANDLADY: How, I should like to know? How?

DOCTOR: Your guitar won't go far, no further than he goes —

LANDLADY: What do you mean by that?

(She catches sight of something on the table)

What's that?

DOCTOR: His payment. A piece of coral.

LANDLADY: Coral?

TALL GRAVEDIGGER: Real coral?

SHORT GRAVEDIGGER: I've never seen coral. Have you ever seen coral?

(The gravediggers come over to the table)

SHORT GRAVEDIGGER: Have you ever seen coral?

LANDLADY: A vagabond like that . . .

(They look at the object)

DOCTOR: He wants to sing a serenade, you see, up at the castle.

LANDLADY: Does he think they'll let him in?

DOCTOR: He thinks so.

LANDLADY: With my guitar! If they let him sit with the servants downstairs in the kitchen, he'll be lucky.

(The sound of music, the Javanese song)

DOCTOR: You hear that? That's the way he feels, a wonderful state, a euphoria, just as the books describe it; everything seems to him so possible and easy, he feels full of life, more so than all of us put together, full of music . . .

LANDLADY: He too?

DOCTOR: He too.

LANDLADY: In a month?

DOCTOR: In a week.

(The Landlady crosses herself)

TALL GRAVEDIGGER: They come from all over the world, but we live by them, I say to myself . . .

LANDLADY: In a week?

DOCTOR: I almost envy him.

LANDLADY: Because he will only live another week?

DOCTOR: Let us say, because he will live for a week . . .

ACT 1

In the castle. The Cavalry Captain is standing, filling his pipe. A Secretary is sitting at the table, on which there are burning candles. A Lad stands waiting.

CAPTAIN: That's all, Kurt. It's a clear case. Let's say no more about it ... Here are your wages.

LAD: Your Honour is dismissing me?

CAPTAIN: We must have order.

(He lights his pipe)

We must have order. You've been my stable lad for eight years —

LAD: Eight and a half.

CAPTAIN: And every day, when you had to fill this pouch, every time, as I learned today, you stole a handful of my tobacco, for eight and a half years.

LAD: Your Honour, I'm sorry.

CAPTAIN: So am I, Kurt.

LAD: I know I shouldn't have done it; and by the way, it wasn't a handful, as Your Honour said, but a pinch, only a pinch, and that makes a difference, Your Honour, after eight and a half years —

CAPTAIN: I liked you. You were a cheerful lad. There aren't many in this household who sing for eight and a half years. Most of them gradually forget how to sing; they imagine that because I can't sing myself I don't like singing . . . You took good care of the horses, I've never had a better stable lad.

LAD: Your Honour used to say that.

CAPTAIN: I'm sorry to have to dismiss you.

LAD: Suppose I returned the tobacco? You could work out how much it came to, over eight and a half years, a pinch every day — and I'd give it back to you in the same brand!

CAPTAIN: It's not a question of the tobacco, young man.

LAD: Then why does Your Honour want to get rid of me, if it's not a question of the tobacco?

CAPTAIN: We must have order.

(In the same tone as at the beginning)

Here are your wages. You can stay here for the night. But tomorrow, as I told you, I don't want to see you around any more.

(The Lad takes his wages and leaves)

CAPTAIN: I'm sorry, but if I forgave him he would think I was only doing so in order to avoid having to look for a new lad, and maybe he'd be right. It would be less troublesome for me, but I'd be doing him a disfavour: he'd start getting impudent. He needs a master he can look up to; he'll never be his own master.

(To the Secretary)

Where were we?

SECRETARY: "Thirdly, as regards the oxen I bought for you, so that you could hitch them to your plough in the spring, and now, because it's winter, none of you want to feed them."

CAPTAIN: I advise you to use your brains, and add a bit of good will so you have enough brains to go round. I have to do that too, if we're to live together, day after day. We'll talk about that when you come to the castle.

(The Secretary is still writing)

That's all — Or add: As regards the foot-rot that is causing us so much worry —

SECRETARY: "That is causing us so much worry . . ."

CAPTAIN: If you let the animals swill schnapps, as I saw you doing recently, and then expect God knows what miracle, that's wasted schnapps! Scrub the animals down, as I told you to, and then drink the schnapps yourself — but first scrub down the cattle!

(He turns away)

That's all for today —

SECRETARY: There's just the journal.

CAPTAIN: Spare me that!

SECRETARY: Your honour, the whole week is empty.

(The Captain sits down)

CAPTAIN: What happens to a man like me in a week? The days are getting shorter, duties fall as thick as snow, I can't even go riding, there's not even the mild excitement of a hare hunt . . . Sunday the such and such, my dear wife's birthday, we had a goose for dinner, it was wonderful . . . Further, dismissed my stable lad . . . Further, we must have order . . .

SECRETARY: "We must have order."

CAPTAIN: Good God, man are you writing?

SECRETARY: "What happens to a Cavalry Captain in a week?"

CAPTAIN: Silence!

SECRETARY: I was quite sure you were telling the truth.

CAPTAIN: Let it stand. But don't read it out to anyone, don't read it out to me... And get to your evening off, it's late again.

(The Secretary gathers up his things, bows and leaves)

CAPTAIN: I can see the Last Judgment. God calls out my name and that rogue of a secretary is standing beside him; "trumpets sound," he reads out loud: "we must have order, we must have order"... he reads it out to all the angels of heaven, to me myself, still pale from dying.

(A servant has entered)

CAPTAIN: What is it now?

SERVANT: Am I disturbing Your Honour?

CAPTAIN: You've brought the wood, that's right.

SERVANT: I thought, it's snowing... outside —

CAPTAIN: Yes, it is, it's been snowing for the last seven days.

SERVANT: And seven nights.

(He stands with the wood in his arms)

It's been snowing for seven days and seven nights. That has never happened before. It's snowing a silence all around that is getting deeper and deeper. It's snowing on the forest, on the paths, it's snowing on every stone and every twig and every post; silence, nothing but silence and snow. For seven days already and seven nights. Wherever you look, it's snowing. It's even snowing on the icicles. And it's snowing on the stream, and everything is falling silent.

(He stares into space)

Your Honour?

CAPTAIN: Yes?

SERVANT: Our well in the courtyard has disappeared —

CAPTAIN: Are you afraid?

SERVANT: Afraid?

(He kneels to make the fire in the fireplace)

Down in the kitchen, we've all been sitting down in the kitchen. Since last Sunday no one has been up to his room, everyone says his room is cold and the snow is blowing in under the tiles, so we're all sleeping down in the kitchen now, the little children sleep in a vegetable basket, while we stay up chatting half the night, and Joseph says it has never gone on snowing for so long before. Seven days and seven nights without a break, that means something, they say, and only the stranger, who sits on the table with his guitar, keeps laughing at us all the time . . .

(He turns round)

Your Honour, that's a very strange man!

CAPTAIN: Who?

SERVANT: The stranger who sits on the table with his guitar and tells us about naked tribes who don't know what snow is, nor fear, nor duties, nor taxes, nor bad teeth. There are such people. And there are mountains that spit sulphur and smoke and red-hot stones up into the blue sky, just like that; he has seen it himself. Our earth is so hot inside. And there are fish that can fly when they want to, and from down under the sea, he says, when you look up, the sun glistens like fragments of green glass . . . He carries a piece of coral in his trouser pocket, Your Honour, we've seen it for ourselves.

CAPTAIN: Who is this fellow? Where does he come from?

SERVANT: From all over the place, so to speak, He has just been telling us about Morocco, about Spain, about Santa Cruz —

CAPTAIN: Santa Cruz?

(The Captain rises)

SERVANT: Yes, he came into the castle six days ago. We thought he was drunk, he didn't even know what he wanted. We laid him down on a bed of straw. But next morning it snowed and snowed. Does Your Honour think it will ever stop again?

(The Captain is standing in front of the globe)

CAPTAIN: Sooner or later everything stops, Kilian.

SERVANT: Everything?

CAPTAIN: Even duties, taxes, bad teeth, foot-rot, oxen — everything — dressing, undressing, eating, the well in the courtyard. One day it will snow unceasingly. The Acropolis, the Bible . . . there will be a silence as though all that had never existed.

SERVANT: The fire is burning. May I go back to the kitchen, Your Honour?

(Elvira has come in)

ELVIRA: It's warmer here . . . Before I forget, Kilian, we'll dine in here, not upstairs.

SERVANT: *(Going)* Very good, My Lady.

(The servant goes out: The Captain and his wife are alone. She crouches by the fireplace, warming her hands: he is still standing in front of the globe)

ELVIRA: It's warmer here. The water is freezing in the vases.

SANTA CRUZ

CAPTAIN: Santa Cruz . . .

ELVIRA: What did you say?

CAPTAIN: Santa Cruz . . . Do you remember Santa Cruz?

ELVIRA: Why?

CAPTAIN: The word is full of strange alleyways and blue sky, full of arches, palms and agaves, walls, masts and sea . . . It smells of fish and seaweed; I see the harbour as dazzling as chalk, as though it were yesterday. I can still hear that fellow in the filthy tavern. We're sailing to Hawaii, he said. Do you see the ship with the red pennant? *(He laughs)* In a quarter of an hour we're setting sail for Hawaii!

ELVIRA: Are you still sorry that you didn't go with him? That you stayed at my side?

CAPTAIN: I often think of that fellow.

ELVIRA: You haven't answered me.

CAPTAIN: I wonder if he has reached Hawaii yet? I often spin this globe around: Florida, Cuba, Java — perhaps he's living in Java now.

ELVIRA: Or he's dead.

CAPTAIN: Not that.

ELVIRA: Perhaps the plague got him.

CAPTAIN: Not that.

ELVIRA: Or war. Or a storm in which he was miserably drowned —

CAPTAIN: Not that.

ELVIRA: Why not?

CAPTAIN: He will live as long as I live.

ELVIRA: *(Looking at him in surprise)* How do you know?

CAPTAIN: As long as I live, my longing will keep him company; he has made it his sail that drives him over the seas, and I, as I sit here, I don't even know where he is roaming with all my longing — while I'm working — ports, shores, cities and I don't know any of them.

ELVIRA: Let him roam!

CAPTAIN: I am letting him . . .

(A brief silence)

ELVIRA: The day after tomorrow is Martinmas. You know our tenants are coming, don't you? We'll give them hot soup — don't you agree?

(He does not hear)

CAPTAIN: Sometimes . . . do you know what I would sometimes like?

ELVIRA: To go to Hawaii.

CAPTAIN: I should like to meet him again, the man who is living my other life. That's all. I should like to know how things have gone with him. I should like to hear about all the things I haven't experienced. I should like to see what my life might have looked like. That's all.

ELVIRA: What a fantasy!

CAPTAIN: It isn't a fantasy. It's a person of flesh and blood who is living on my strength, feeding on my longing; otherwise I shouldn't always be so tired, so old.

ELVIRA: Are you old and tired then?

CAPTAIN: Often, too often.

ELVIRA: *(Joking)* Perhaps it's the vagabond who is singing down in the kitchen, the fellow who entertains our servants with coral and a guitar? My chambermaid told me about it. Perhaps it's him!

CAPTAIN: Perhaps.

ELVIRA: That's enough of that!

(Elvira stands up)

Is the snow making you all mad? My chambermaid dreams of fish that can fly.

(A brief silence)

CAPTAIN: When I sit beside you in the evening after the day's work is done, for example, when I read — what else are we looking for but the one who is living our other life, perhaps our more real life, the life I should now be living if I had gone aboard the foreign ship that time, if I had chosen the sea and not the land, the vast and terrifying, not the cosy and safe. I was looking for the one, of whom I can't help thinking all the time, even when I rejoice in our happiness . . . in our child, our land, when it is summer, in the early morning when I ride through the fields and look at the crops, in the evening when the twilight clouds drift over the corn, our corn — God, I know that I am happy!

ELVIRA: I thought you were.

CAPTAIN: All this here — I no longer believe it is the only life I could have lived. Do you understand?

ELVIRA: What do you believe then?

CAPTAIN: Once I did believe that absolutely, as long as it was still a goal, not fulfilment, not possession, not everyday life.

ELVIRA: Then you don't believe in God any more either.

CAPTAIN: Why do you say that?

ELVIRA: That's how it seems to me. My dear father once wrote in a letter: Don't be afraid of chance. If you marry a pirate or a cavalry captain, your life will look rather different; but you will always be Elvira . . . I felt abashed when I read it, but at the same time filled with confidence, and what chance brought next was a cavalry captain, as you know, and I said yes . . . That was in Santa Cruz.

CAPTAIN: About seventeen years ago . . . Oh, here's Kilian again. It's time I changed, I suppose.

(He stands up)

We're dining up here, you said?

(The servant has come in and is laying table)

ELVIRA: One more thing, Kilian —

SERVANT: Yes, My Lady?

ELVIRA: Lay a third place.

CAPTAIN: Who are you expecting?

ELVIRA: And tell the stranger down in the kitchen that, although we don't know him, we're expecting him to dinner — here.

SERVANT: The vagabond?

ELVIRA: We're expecting him as our guest.

SERVANT: As Your Ladyship wishes.

(Servant leaves)

CAPTAIN: What's the idea of that?

ELVIRA: Didn't you say you wanted to meet him?

CAPTAIN: You're a fool!

ELVIRA: I thought I was doing you a favour. We shall meet your other life, as you call it. It will be an interesting dinner.

(Elvira has sat down at the clavichord)

Seriously, my dear husband, how would you feel if I gave myself up to memories the way you do? If I talked like that about an Elvira who lived my other life, perhaps my more real life — far from here?

CAPTAIN: People say that women can more easily forget.

ELVIRA: So they say. I haven't forgotten. His name was Pelegrin —

(A brief silence)

But, you see, women don't play with love, with marriage, with fidelity, with the man they have followed.

CAPTAIN: Do I play?

ELVIRA: What has happened in the past is over and done with, it has no further right to my present, no place in my thoughts! When a woman says, Yes, I will follow you, then she acts according to her "Yes," sacrifices everything else, doesn't think about it any more, has no regrets. I have done that. Because I love. I should like the man who is everything to me to have something entire and whole in me too.

CAPTAIN: I believe you, Elvira. I know that is true.

(He gives her a marital kiss)

And I envy you such fidelity. I can achieve it in deed, God knows — but not in spirit.

(The Servant comes back, lays the third place, while the Captain is leaving)

ELVIRA: Have you invited him?

SERVANT: Certainly, My Lady.

ELVIRA: Is he coming?

SERVANT: We shall see.

ELVIRA: He will feel embarrassed, the poor fellow!

SERVANT: Does Your Ladyship think so?

ELVIRA: People who don't belong to the gentry have such extraordinary ideas about them.

(Elvira toys with the clavichord)

SERVANT: Your Ladyship?

ELVIRA: Yes?

SERVANT: Our well in the courtyard has disappeared.

(Then he continues laying the table)

I suppose the guest will sit here. If he comes. Because, if you will permit me to say so, he appears to me to be drunk.

ELVIRA: Drunk?

SERVANT: Not terribly, My Lady, not blind drunk. But all the same.

ELVIRA: All the same? How much is "all the same?"

SERVANT: I say that so Your Ladyship knows why I'm not putting out the Venetian glasses —

ELVIRA: Why not?

SERVANT: The fellow — our guest . . . it's a habit of his to throw the glass in the corner as soon as it's empty, every time he empties one.

ELVIRA: Wonderful . . .

SERVANT: If Your Ladyship says so.

ELVIRA: Kilian!

SERVANT: Yes?

ELVIRA: I want the Venetian glasses on the table.

SERVANT: They're our best, My Lady; the Captain loves them more than anything, they remind him of his travels, of the sea —

ELVIRA: That's why I want them.

(The Vagabond is standing in the doorway unobserved, while Elvira tinkles on the clavichord and the Servant continues laying the table)

ELVIRA: Kilian, what does this guest of ours looks like?

SERVANT: What does he look like?

ELVIRA: Describe him! Has he a beard like a tramp? I imagine his hair hangs down over his collar, as though barbers were extinct.

SERVANT: He has no collar.

ELVIRA: When I was a child I once saw a tramp who was drinking soup and using his beard to wipe his mouth — ugh!

SERVANT: Our guest has no beard.

ELVIRA: Pity.

SERVANT: Nonetheless Your Ladyship is in for a surprise.

ELVIRA: What about his shoes? Tell me about his shoes. Have you ever seen the shoes the gypsies leave lying in the brown puddles when they move on?

SERVANT: Yes, pretty much like that.

ELVIRA: Poor fellow! We'll give him a pair of shoes afterwards.

SERVANT: That would be noble of Your Ladyship.

ELVIRA: Afterwards! You understand. The Captain wants to get to know him just as he is . . . Drunk, did you say?

SERVANT: I'm afraid Your Ladyship isn't going to enjoy this dinner very much.

ELVIRA: On the contrary.

SERVANT: I mean, he's really poor.

ELVIRA: Oh, I'm not the sort of person who dislikes the poor.

SERVANT: I mean he has nothing to lose. People like that have a way of speaking the truth —

ELVIRA: What kind of truth?

SERVANT: Any truth that comes into his head. It isn't difficult to be courageous when you're already down and out.

ELVIRA: I value the truth.

SERVANT: Even when it's shocking? He has been through a good deal, I believe.

ELVIRA: For example?

SERVANT: For example, he has been in prison.

ELVIRA: In prison?

SERVANT: I expect women had something to do with it . . .

ELVIRA: He has been in prison, you say?

SERVANT: So he says.

ELVIRA: Wonderful!

SERVANT: They were going to hang him, I believe.

ELVIRA: Wonderful, quite wonderful.

SERVANT: Why does Your Ladyship find that wonderful?

ELVIRA: Why?

(She turns back to the clavichord)

Because it will drive the fancies and obsessions out of the head of a man who isn't satisfied with his destiny — that's why.

(Elvira tinkles on the clavichord, the Servant leaves, in the doorway he meets the guest)

SERVANT: Your Ladyship. The guest.

ELVIRA: Ah! Has the gong rung then? . . .

(Elvira turns round to greet the guest; she is turned to stone when she sees him)

VAGABOND: Good evening, Elvira.

ELVIRA: Pelegrin?

PELEGRIN: I've been invited to dinner, I believe.

ELVIRA: Pelegrin . . .

(Silence)

PELEGRIN: Don't be frightened, Elvira; I shall go again soon, I haven't much time.

(Silence)

You have a beautiful home, just as I always imagined . . . only I think that log ought to be pushed further into the fireplace — if you will permit me.

(He takes the poker)

You're surprised that I should have come to this impossible district, Elvira . . . I was ill, fever, fever, as though hell were burning in my blood. Now I'm well again. Such things happen: I'm better than I've ever been!

(He stands up again in front of the fire)

In Cuba there is a farm, burnt down and dried up, a farm that is waiting for me in order to bear fruit: pineapples, peaches, plums, figs, grapes! The ship sails in a month . . . In a year, Elvira, you will receive the first lot of coffee!

(Elvira, who all this time has stood as mute as a post, suddenly turns round, gathers up her skirt and makes off in resolute flight)

PELEGRIN: Why are you running away? I didn't mean to frighten you . . . So that's your child.

(He stands in front of a picture)

You look a little like your mother. Eyes almost like the eyes of a deer. Maybe your mother is weeping now, with anger — I've reminded her of things you're not supposed to know about; a man is nothing but a fool and life is short, that above all.

(He looks round)

And all these books . . .

(As he picks one up)

One day, I don't know when, I shall read you, all of you, you beautiful honeycombs filled with the spirit of centuries, spattered with candle wax.

(The Captain appears: he is taken aback by the behaviour of his guest, who is in no way disturbed, but continues to leaf through the books throughout the following)

CAPTAIN: God be with you!

PELEGRIN: And with you . . . It seems Your Honour is also a lover of engravings? You collect, an amiable little vice.

CAPTAIN: My wife will be here in a moment.

PELEGRIN: Do you think so?

CAPTAIN: They tell me you've been in our house almost a week; the snow held you prisoner.

PELEGRIN: That too.

CAPTAIN: We seldom have so much snow.

PELEGRIN: I used to collect too once — Red Indian skulls, over in America. The devil knows how they do it; they're this size, as big as a fist, real human heads. Dead of course. But perfectly preserved, the flesh, the skin, the eyes, the hair, even the individual's features, only all shrunken! On the farm, where I was working at the time, I had a whole rack full of those gentlemen: you can hold them in your hand like a potato — one day the women annoyed me and I threw heads at them till I had none left!

(He laughs)

Why are you looking at me like that?

CAPTAIN: I have the feeling we've met before somewhere . . .

PELEGRIN: Have we?

CAPTAIN: I don't know; do you remember me?

(Servant enters)

SERVANT: The mistress sends her apologies. She has migraine, she says, or stomach ache.

CAPTAIN: Thank you.

(The servant goes)

Let us sit down.

(They sit)

PELEGRIN: I believe it was in Santa Cruz . . . *(Captain hands him food)* Thank you . . . It was in Santa Cruz. *(Captain hands him more food)* Thank you . . . It was in Santa Cruz, in that damn tavern, where they stole my silver amulet.

CAPTAIN: Who did?

PELEGRIN: The negroes! Do you remember the negro who sold oysters? I still maintain they stank . . . Thanks . . . I waited for you aboard our ship; didn't you say you were coming with us? The ship with the red pennant. Do you remember?

CAPTAIN: I remember very clearly.

PELEGRIN: *Viola,* she was called.

CAPTAIN: — *Viola?*

PELEGRIN: What a voyage that was! Off Madagascar the French nabbed us. For nine weeks we sat in jail gnawing our nails; we ate the mould off the walls! Fortunately I fell ill — we were condemned to the galleys. Pirates! But first, so that I should be fit to be damned, they took me to hospital. A nurse gave me blood . . . Yes, they do that, you know. She rolled up her white sleeve, sat there and gave me blood . . . Later I jumped off the pier with it and swam — I mean I swam with the nurse's blood — I swam and swam; it was a moonlit night and there was a Dutch merchantman lying offshore that was just weighing anchor. I could hear the anchor-chain rattling already. — Excuse me.

CAPTAIN: What's the matter?

PELEGRIN: You don't say a word.

CAPTAIN: I'm listening . . .

PELEGRIN: I keep on chattering away, and you're not even eating. I'm not being polite.

CAPTAIN: I like listening, really. Don't be put off by my curiosity to hear about all the things I haven't experienced in my life.

PELEGRIN: Let us clink glasses! I'm not being polite.

(They clink glasses)

To your wife!

(They drink)

Later we came to Hawaii ...

(They are about to go on eating, but suddenly music is heard: they listen, look at one another, and listen, holding their napkins)

CAPTAIN: What's that music?

PELEGRIN: Music ...

CAPTAIN: Where is it coming from?

PELEGRIN: That's what the sailors, those brown devils with cat's eyes, always used to sing when we lay up on the quarterdeck and couldn't sleep for the heat, all night long, all those nights without wind ...

CAPTAIN: Where is it coming from?

(A young girl is standing in the doorway)

VIOLA: Father.

CAPTAIN: What has happened?

VIOLA: I don't know.

CAPTAIN: Something has happened ...

VIOLA: Mama is crying, she doesn't say why.

CAPTAIN: May I introduce our daughter?

PELEGRIN: God be with you!

CAPTAIN: Her name is Viola.

PELEGRIN: Viola . . . ?

(The stage goes dark, but the music continues, the sailors' song comes closer and closer)

ACT 2

On the quarterdeck. It is night, the sailors are lying around singing the song that has just been talked about; suddenly they stop.

FIRST SAILOR: The wind's in no hurry.

SECOND SAILOR: The wind's got plenty of time . . .

THIRD SAILOR: Our barrels are stinking to high heaven!

FIRST SAILOR: The moon hangs like a silver gong over the sea.

SECOND SAILOR: It seems to me the moon is hanging like a lantern between the masts.

THIRD SAILOR: Pedro? Pedro?

FIRST SAILOR: He's asleep. He doesn't feel the irons when he's asleep.

THIRD SAILOR: Hey, Pedro?

PEDRO: I'm not asleep.

FIRST SAILOR: Pedro, what's new in the land of fairy stories?

PEDRO: You don't believe a word I say, and yet you always want me to tell you stories, you maddening rabble, who clap me in irons when I tell you the unadulterated truth!

FIRST SAILOR: Easy, my friend —

PEDRO: Who laid me flat on my face for three nights on end, so that I shouldn't see the stars?

SECOND SAILOR: You shouldn't tell us the stars are singing. When we can't hear a sound. It isn't true, what you tell us. That's why we clapped you in irons.

PEDRO: If what I tell you isn't true, why do you want me to tell you things at all? Why do you listen?

FIRST SAILOR: Because we're bored . . .

PEDRO: And why are you bored?

THIRD SAILOR: He's a poet! Let him be.

SECOND SAILOR: That's what I can't stand, all that damn rubbish! He's always talking about things I can't see with my own eyes. We'll sail you around the whole earth until we can see that what you tell us is true — just one of all your stories! Then we'll set you free.

PEDRO: Once you see what's true?

THIRD SAILOR: Not a moment earlier! Don't laugh!

PEDRO: Once you blind men see! You people with your incurable certainty you're right, just because you're in the majority, you ghastly gang with the shameless demand that springs from your dreariness and boredom, you empty vessels, you bottomless barrels, you public! . . .

(Laughter and noise)

I'll never tell you any more stories. Never again.

THIRD SAILOR: I demand a penalty of three days without bread.

SECOND SAILOR: Three days with no water.

MAJORITY: Agreed.

(A voice from another part of the ship sings the song again)

PEDRO: Seventeen years ago, I tell you, and on this very ship, he abducted her; her name was Elvira, a lady, I tell you, a young lady, and he carried her into that cabin there, whether you believe me or not; that's where it happened —

SECOND SAILOR: What?

PEDRO: Seventeen years ago . . .

THIRD SAILOR: Lies, lies, nothing but lies!

PEDRO: Now she is the wife of a cavalry captain; she lives in a castle, far from here, on the other side of the world, where it's winter now. We can't sleep for the heat, and there, you must picture it to yourselves, they're sitting by the fireside, the cavalry captain and his wife. They don't know what to talk about, they've been married so long. A servant comes in. What is it? asks the captain. There's a vagabond in the house. They invite him to dinner, they're so bored, and when the captain's wife sees who it is — what do you think she does?

FIRST SAILOR: Well who is it?

PEDRO: Our skipper! Who else?

THIRD SAILOR: Lies, lies, nothing but lies!

PEDRO: What do you think the cavalry captain's wife does when she sees who it is coming up from the basement of her husband's castle? She turns away, without a word.

FIRST SAILOR: Why?

PEDRO: The cavalry captain and the vagabond sit at the table alone; they eat and drink; they chat about times gone by, and all of a sudden they hear music. What's that music? asks the cavalry captain.

SECOND SAILOR: What is it?

PEDRO: Well, it's the song we were just singing, what else could it be?

SECOND SAILOR: How is that possible?

PEDRO: Memory, friends, memory; distance is no defence against memory; the cavalry captain's wife hears our song, even if she is at the other end of the world, where it's winter now, where it's snowing; she is lying in the bedroom of her husband's castle, the good woman, she is weeping into her pillow; she doesn't want to be reminded of what happened here in the cabin seventeen years ago — on account of fidelity...

FIRST SAILOR: I can imagine!

SECOND SAILOR: On account of fidelity!

PEDRO: Only sometimes in dreams —

THIRD SAILOR: Lies, I say. All lies!

PEDRO: Only sometimes in dreams he comes back, the seducer from the past, impudent as he was, young as he was, at that time... It was a night like tonight, the silver moon casting its path on the sea. He brings her over here once more, she is dreaming she's still a girl, dreaming she loses her innocence once more...

SECOND SAILOR: Wonderful! Do you hear what the cavalry captain's wife dreams about? How she is losing her innocence once more?

FIRST SAILOR: Nothing's more powerful than innocence and thirst; you can do so much with them.

THIRD SAILOR: Lies, nothing but rotten lies!

PEDRO: Quiet.

THIRD SAILOR: Lies, I say. All lies.

PEDRO: Here they come — behind us...

(Elvira appears, in her silk nightdress, accompanied by Pelegrin, looking as he might have looked seventeen years ago)

PELEGRIN: One more step.

ELVIRA: I mustn't stumble, otherwise I shall wake up.

PELEGRIN: I'm holding you.

(They come down)

PEDRO: I'm sorry for the cavalry captain, who can't see all this behind the forehead of his sleeping wife . . .

(The singing has stopped)

PELEGRIN: On your feet, men! What are you doing lying around singing? Why don't any of you jump up when I come? What's the meaning of this? Get a move on, hoist the sails! We're putting to sea. Are you dreaming?

(The sailors stand up in a daze)

We're setting sail! At once! Understand!

(The sailors set to work; only Pedro, who is in irons, is left lying in the dark)

ELVIRA: So this is your ship?

PELEGRIN: Her name is *Viola*, yes —

ELVIRA: *Viola?*

PELEGRIN: A wretched thing, it's true. We seized her the other day, when she was lying off the coast of Morocco; the crew were all drunk; she didn't cost us much — the lives of three of our men, she's not worth more — but she'll do, she's a ship in which I can sail out with Elvira to a place where there's nothing left but the moon and the sea, the sea . . .

ELVIRA: This is where you said I was beautiful.

PELEGRIN: You *are* beautiful, Elvira!

ELVIRA: You said it differently . . . then.

PELEGRIN: I know a sea shell that doesn't exist, a shell you can only imagine, it's so beautiful, and if you walked along all the shores of all the seas and if you opened up thousands and hundreds of thousands of shells, all of them together wouldn't be as beautiful as the shell you can only imagine — but you are as beautiful!

ELVIRA: Oh Pelegrin!

(She swoons; he holds her, sets her on a barrel)

PELEGRIN: Jehu!

ELVIRA: I'm not cold. Really I'm not.

PELEGRIN: Jehu!

ELVIRA: I don't want them to bring the red rug.

PELEGRIN: Jehu! Where the hell has he got to? Jehu!

ELVIRA: I'm not thirsty. I shall never drink your yellow wine again. Never! Do you hear, Pelegrin? I won't —

(A young Malay appears)

PELEGRIN: Bring the girl who is our guest a rug. Bring us fruit, bring us food, bring us wine, bring us the best — bring us everything there is!

(The young Malay leaves)

I can't help laughing when I think of your father! Such a stern gentleman! I told his servant what to say to him tomorrow morning when he gets out of bed. Do you see that little ship with the red pennant far out to sea? the servant will ask him. I can't see anything, your father will say. And the servant will answer: I can't see anything any more either.

ELVIRA: My poor father; I'm so sorry for him because of his daughter.

PELEGRIN: One shouldn't go around telling every young man: I have a pearl of a daughter, but you, my lads, aren't good enough to look at her! Where is she then? I asked. That's none of your business, he growled. She's engaged.

ELVIRA: He was right.

PELEGRIN: She's engaged, he said, and the pride, oh the pride trickled from the corners of his mouth as he added: to a nobleman, a cavalry captain!

ELVIRA: Seriously, Pelegrin —

PELEGRIN: Seriously, I've been sailing after you for thirteen weeks —

(A strange sing-song of shouts rings out)

ELVIRA: What's that?

PELEGRIN: I couldn't think of any other way to see you again; I needed a ship, the first one I could lay my hands on . . . I can still hear the sinister splash; the poor Frenchies, we chucked them overboard; drunk as they were, splash, splash, splash! We painted over the coat of arms —

ELVIRA: What's that?

PELEGRIN: They're hoisting the sail. They do it to a rhythm. I bet that as soon as the moon has disappeared we shall have wind! And when you wake up tomorrow you'll see what a morning we shall have, a morning full of jubilant sunshine, a morning full of blue skies and wind, a morning without shores, limitless —

ELVIRA: I know what it will be like, Pelegrin, we have lived through it before.

(The young Malay brings a basket in the style of Titian)

ELVIRA: My God, my God!

PELEGRIN: I don't think we shall be bored till dawn breaks. I love fruit. It always makes me pious. It seems to me that when God made fruit he did a good job . . . Jehu, we thank you!

(The young Malay leaves)

PELEGRIN: I love that lad, he walks as though his feet never touched the ground, he has the eyes of a sorrowful beast, he has a voice like velvet, when he laughs . . .

(He tries to clink glasses)

To our health!

ELVIRA: I don't drink wine.

PELEGRIN: The wine is good. One must give the Frenchies credit for that.

ELVIRA: Never again, Pelegrin, never again!

PELEGRIN: It's good wine. You have to give the Frenchies credit for that.

ELVIRA: Never again, Pelegrin, never again.

PELEGRIN: Why not?

(He tries to clink glasses)

Let us drink before it's spilt.

(Elvira does not raise her glass)

The wine you spurn on such a night as this is more dangerous than if you drink it!

ELVIRA: Why?

PELEGRIN: I should be bound to think: the girl's afraid. And what of? I should be bound to ask myself, what is she afraid of? Such a question gives a man audacious ideas, and in the end, if you don't drink, in the end he will actually imagine that the girl has the same ideas.

(Elvira takes the glass)

To our health!

(He drinks, Elvira looks into her glass)

ELVIRA: Why do I dream all that over and over again? I know perfectly well that later you will abandon me, you will behave like a scoundrel. I know all that, because I have lived through it. Many years ago. And all that is over and done with, over and done with for ever, and yet I never cease to relive it. Later I shall marry a cavalry captain; it's funny how clearly I know that: I am lying in the bedroom of our castle, and at this moment, he, the good man, comes up, he is looking at my sleeping face — at this moment . . .

(A lookout approaches them)

LOOKOUT: Sir!

PELEGRIN: What is it, you slinking dog?

LOOKOUT: A corvette!

PELEGRIN: Where?

LOOKOUT: To port.

PELEGRIN: What do they want?

LOOKOUT: We have no coat of arms, sir, they think we're pirates.

PELEGRIN: May be.

LOOKOUT: Sir, they'll fire on us as soon as dawn breaks.

ELVIRA: They'll fire on us?

(Pelegrin empties his glass and throws it overboard)

PELEGRIN: Of course they'll fire on us. We must have order. What else could they possibly do? . . . Tell the crew: every man to his station! When the trouble starts in earnest I shall be on the bridge!

LOOKOUT: Very good, sir.

(The lookout goes)

PELEGRIN: Let us go into the cabin, dear Elvira. The moon will help us by going down. It won't be the first time we have given them the slip.

ELVIRA: Pelegrin, I'm not going into the cabin.

PELEGRIN: Why not?

ELVIRA: Never again, Pelegrin, never again!

PELEGRIN: What do you mean by that? I don't understand . . .

ELVIRA: I'm not going into the cabin! Not for anything in the world!

PELEGRIN: That's the best place, believe me, the safest. You will have a bed, the only one on our ship, and when it's over I'll wake you.

ELVIRA: And then?

PELEGRIN: It may be dangerous up here. The quarterdeck is no place for you! I know them, those idiots over there: they take life so seriously, the lives of others, of course, the lives they envy, because they never manage to have one of their own . . . they're so bloodthirsty about it . . .

(Because Elvira doesn't follow him:) Why are you staring at me like that?

ELVIRA: I'm believing you again as I did then.

PELEGRIN: Believing what?

ELVIRA: Later, when I kept thinking back on that night, it always seemed to me that it was all a trick on your part, a ruse, with the cabin and all that, a dirty, low-down ruse —

PELEGRIN: Elvira, we must go, I beseech you!

ELVIRA: Oh Pelegrin . . .

PELEGRIN: You'll be safe in the cabin. And alone.

ELVIRA: I know what happened in the cabin — when the shooting was over . . . seventeen years ago . . .

(She screams)

My God! Who is this man lying here in irons?

PEDRO: It's me.

PELEGRIN: Pedro?

PEDRO: I can't help it, sir. They put me in irons, the unbelievers!

ELVIRA: Great God, he has been listening to us . . .

PELEGRIN: He's only a poet whom no one will believe when he talks . . . Come, Elvira, come! Let us go to the cabin, you'll be safest there.

(The sound of a canon)

They're firing their guns already, those idiots of order —

(She falls into his arms)

ELVIRA: All that, all that. Why do I keep dreaming it over and over again?

(He carries her into the cabin)

PEDRO: And the cavalry captain can't see any of that, behind the forehead of his sleeping wife . . .

ACT 3

In the castle. The Secretary is sitting at the table as before. Luggage is standing on the floor. The Servant is waiting beside it.

SECRETARY: It's past midnight.

SERVANT: I don't understand what it means...

SECRETARY: I've been seventeen years in his service, never a mood, never a caprice, I had my free evenings, my night's rest, my human dignity. Yesterday evening, as I sat at this table, I would still have staked my head that the Captain, our master, was a man of sense, a man of decorum, a man who knew the value of having a secretary like me. How often have I said to him: if necessary, Your Honour, I will work all through the night — and I could be sure that he wouldn't take advantage of the offer.

SERVANT: Ssh!

(They listen)

That's the vagabond.

SECRETARY: Is he still awake too then?

SERVANT: I ran into him just now, while I was taking the trunks down from the loft. No thanks, he said, when I offered to show him his room. He didn't want to sleep, he said, it was a pity to waste the time, he said. He would look at the pictures.

SECRETARY: Idiot!

(Secretary yawns)

SERVANT: Do you know what I think?

SECRETARY: I'm supposed to write a letter — in the middle of the night.

SERVANT: It's all the fault of the vagabond. That's what I think. It started with our mistress's stomach-ache. Then they drank until midnight, the Captain and the vagabond. They cracked nuts, just look at these piles of shells, and they kept calling for another bottle.

SECRETARY: I'm freezing to death.

SERVANT: Can a man who has a castle, a wife, a child just go off like that? The day after tomorrow is Martinmas and who is going to deal with the tenants when they come? Tell me that. What's going to happen to the oxen? And who is going to pay our wages? I can't believe that a cavalry captain can just go off like that, as though he were the only person who existed.

SECRETARY: Suppose longing is pulling him, harder than the two oxen?

SERVANT: That's a bachelor speaking. What does a bachelor know, even if he has been around the world! . . .

SECRETARY: Don't talk poppycock, Kilian — you're making me yawn!

SERVANT: A bachelor knows nothing about such things.

SECRETARY: I'll answer you tomorrow.

SERVANT: I can't believe that a cavalry captain can do whatever he has a mind to.

SECRETARY: First he was going to set out in his nightshirt. I pointed it out to him. Quite right, he growled, quite right, it's winter, it's always winter in this country.

SERVANT: That's an exaggeration.

SECRETARY: Now he has gone to change his clothes. He wants to put on the jerkin of his youth again, he says.

SERVANT: What does he want to put on?

SECRETARY: The jerkin of his youth. That's why it's taking so long. He's going to find it difficult . . .

SERVANT: I don't understand all that.

SECRETARY: My friend, there are things that don't happen so that we can understand them. But they happen just the same. It's called madness —

SERVANT: Quiet!

(The Cavalry Captain appears in the jerkin of his youth)

CAPTAIN: Is the sledge ready?

SERVANT: Certainly, Your Honour.

CAPTAIN: Are the horses harnessed?

SERVANT: Certainly, Your Honour.

CAPTAIN: The trunks on the sledge?

SERVANT: Waiting for Your Honour to give the word.

CAPTAIN: Kilian!

SERVANT: Yes?

CAPTAIN: Softly. No one must wake up. It's night. Our mistress is sleeping. And dreaming —

(The servant carries the trunks out)

CAPTAIN: Where did we leave off?

SERVANT: "To my wife, written at the moment of departure, which could not be delayed, because I became aware of the shortness of our lives, at one o'clock in the morning. Dearest Elvira, since you cannot know that I know, and since I, for my part, cannot know where you are this night, where you have travelled to with the strange man whose name I have heard three times from your lips, I am writing this letter to you while you are apparently asleep up there in our bedroom, as you have slept all these years. I shall leave this on the dining-room table in case, in the morning, you come down to breakfast again, as you always do, as though nothing had happened, and find yourself alone, about which I am truly sorry. This night, as I stood beside you, I heard a sweetness in your voice, dearest Elvira, such as I have never heard before in any woman's voice — "

CAPTAIN: The belt seems to have got twisted. *(He throws it away)* I heard a sweetness in your voice such as I have never heard before in any woman's voice . . . yes.

SECRETARY: That's as far as we got.

CAPTAIN: No comments . . . Write: Under these circumstances I feel that my longing, which for years I have killed, have killed and buried in silence, for fear it would frighten you, dearest Elvira, I feel that my longing too is entitled to go on a journey.

SECRETARY: ". . . is entitled to go on a journey."

(The Captain who has been striding up and down the room while he dictated stops; he speaks to himself or to Elvira)

CAPTAIN: To see the sea again . . . Do you understand what I mean? Once again the limitless expanse of the possible; not to know what the next moment will bring, a word that draws one to the other end of the world, a ship, a chance meeting, a conversation in a tavern, someone said: Hawaii! And when you wake the splashing of the waves is all around you, nothing but the sky, nothing but the curved surfaces of the water; there are continents anchored amid this expanse of water, and those I love, those I think of in the lonely jubilation of such an hour, are all far away, they are on the same planet that drifts, all in flower, through the darkness of the universe — yes, they are walking down below, with their feet to my feet!

SECRETARY: Softly, Your Honour...

CAPTAIN: Ever since I talked to that stranger how clearly I have felt that we are mortal! Before us endless time, the sombre mindlessness of things, the emptiness of a God who erupts out of volcanoes, rises in mist from the sea, blossoms and withers, rots away and turns into coal and blossoms again in primeval forests, a God who has no eye with which to look at his unending summers — but we, his only hope of being looked at, of being mirrored in the gleam of a mortal human eye, we, that improbable instant called humanity, we, that special case of a unique, a slowly cooling planet... and I myself, a spark of this cosmic instant, capable of feeling this, of knowing it, of living it —

SECRETARY: Softly, softly!

CAPTAIN: Elvira, I want to live again, to be able to weep again, to be able to laugh, to be able to love again and thrill at the perfume of a night, to be able to exult. We scarcely remember what that was like; they were only moments in years. I should like to be able to feel again what a blessing it is to be alive, to be alive as I draw this breath — before we are buried under the snow to all eternity.

(The servant comes back)

SERVANT: Your Honour, the sledge is ready.

(The servant goes again)

CAPTAIN: Where had we got to?

SECRETARY: "Under these circumstances . . . etc., dearest Elvira, I feel that my longing too is entitled to go on a journey."

CAPTAIN: Before we are buried under the snow to all eternity.

(The Captain goes, while the Secretary is still writing)

SECRETARY: " — before we are buried under the snow to all eternity."

(He sprinkles sand over the letter)

So I was right . . . that damned vagabond! He wanders around the house cracking nuts and looking at the pictures, the miserable hypocrite, and meanwhile, up in the bedroom, he is sailing across all the seas of dreams with our mistress . . . abducting her once again on the ship of memory . . .

(Pelegrin has been standing in the doorway as the Secretary was speaking; he is cracking and chewing nuts, which he takes from his trouser pocket)

PELEGRIN: It's still snowing outside.

SECRETARY: Well, well! I was just cursing you, yes, you and no one else!

PELEGRIN: Why?

SECRETARY: Tell me, my dear sir, do you know what you've done tonight?

PELEGRIN: I? What?

SECRETARY: You vagabond, you ghost from the past, what are you up to? Because of you I was woken in the middle of the night. What are you after, I should like to know? What are you doing in the dreams of a married woman?

PELEGRIN: I?

SECRETARY: You don't even blush . . .

PELEGRIN: I don't know what you're talking about. *(Cracking nuts)* Wonderful nuts you have here!

(The Secretary gathers his things together)

SECRETARY: I know what's going on. Look at this letter! In the middle of the night . . . Do you really think you can jumble up time just as you like? This is an orderly house, do you understand! What is past is past. Yesterday, today, tomorrow! You turn the pages of the years this way and that, forwards and backwards — what a mess you make!

PELEGRIN: I don't understand what you're so angry about.

SECRETARY: Just wait till our mistress wakes up. She won't thank you, she'll tell you —

PELEGRIN: What?

(Sleigh bells)

SECRETARY: There! Do you hear that? He's off, in the middle of the night, off and away —

PELEGRIN: Who?

SECRETARY: The Captain.

PELEGRIN: Where to?

(Throughout the following the silvery ringing of sleigh-bells is heard gradually fading away into the distance)

Outside it's still snowing. The snow is creating a silence all round that is growing deeper and deeper. It's snowing on the forest, on the roofs, it's snowing on every path and every twig and every post. Silence, nothing but silence and snow. Wherever you look, it's snowing. It's even snowing on the icicles. It's snowing on the stream, and one day everything will have fallen silent.

SECRETARY: I'm going to bed.

PELEGRIN: Do that.

SECRETARY: What about you, why don't you go to bed?

PELEGRIN: I'm waiting.

SECRETARY: Are you waiting for our mistress?

PELEGRIN: Don't disturb her, so long as she is dreaming. Don't wake her.

(The secretary goes: Pelegrin stands by the window)

I don't think I have very much longer to live . . . In a few hours dawn will break.

ACT 4

In Santa Cruz.

PEDRO: Santa Cruz . . . palms and agaves, walls, masts, sea. Every now and then a noise from the harbour, the sound of singing from somewhere . . . So this is the tavern in Santa Cruz as it must have looked then. Seventeen years ago! It still smells of fish. Down by the jetty, where our ship lies at anchor, the water is as green as a bottle, there's a rotten melon floating on it, and perhaps a patch of shimmering oil. And so on. Then too, I believe, it was a day like this, as dazzling as chalk, the shadows like ink. Up above an expanse of sky, cloudless, of course. I don't know what those birds are. And from time to time, in the midst of the blue peacefulness filled with singing, a chain rattles a chain . . . That's all Santa Cruz as we remember it later. The nigger is there too!

(The Negro enters selling oysters)

NEGRO: Hey, hey! Hey, hey!

PEDRO: I like his simple outlook on life.

NEGRO: What's this I see?

PEDRO: Although he's a crook. He was the one who stole the silver amulet, while Pelegrin was scuffling with him. We might wonder: why was Pelegrin scuffling with him? We shall see —

NEGRO: Why are you in irons?

PEDRO: Because.

NEGRO: I was going to say: Fresh oysters, sir! But how could you eat oysters when you're in irons? I can't do business with you . . . they tell me you're a poet!

(The Negro grins and walks on)

PEDRO: I love his simple mind. He believes in God the way we taught him. One must do right. But what is right? It could be there is no right. As it was in our story, as it so often is between a man and a woman. Whatever they do, Elvira and Pelegrin, it's bound to be painful. What have they done to deserve that? Because they love one another, a man and a woman, as God created them for one another, so that they could make each other guilty. This is the world of a God whom we call "loving", because he has mercy on us — afterwards . . .

(Elvira and Pelegrin have appeared)

PELEGRIN: It's shady here.

ELVIRA: I can't go any further.

PELEGRIN: I can't understand why you're always crying, my dear. Not a day passes without your crying. Who said anything about leaving you? I implore you, who is going to leave you?

ELVIRA: You.

PELEGRIN: How can you talk like that?

ELVIRA: You will leave me — when you sail away.

PELEGRIN: I shan't sail without you!

ELVIRA: Pelegrin, I'm not sailing any further.

(Pedro is sitting in the foreground)

PEDRO: It's the old story. They love each other, no doubt about it, and they will have to leave each other, no doubt about that either. That's what is so senseless. Believe it or not: a time comes when there is no solution any more.

(Elvira has sat down. Pelegrin is standing in front of her)

PELEGRIN: Do you really think I'm a scoundrel? That I shall take you into this tavern and suddenly make off, raise the anchor and leave you sitting there? Here among negroes and sailors? Do you think that? Do you think I shall slip away like a thief, an adventurer, for whom you were no more than a glass of wine that a man drains and leaves standing, not caring if it falls in pieces . . .

(To Pedro)

Pedro, where's our crew? Tell them to hurry. Tell them to call us as soon as the ship is ready.

PEDRO: I'll tell them that.

PELEGRIN: Why are you in irons? Again.

PEDRO: A silly joke. I tell them a story, they set me free as soon as they see that it's true. But of course the moment the majority see the story is true, the real truth lies further on, and when I tell them this they once more refuse to believe me until they see it, and then they clap me in irons again.

PELEGRIN: What kind of story?

PEDRO: An old story, friend —

PELEGRIN: This is no time for old stories, tell them to call me as soon as our ship is ready.

(Pedro stays where he is)

We must move on. Devil take this Santa Cruz! All the thirteen days our ship has been anchored down there, I have trembled every instant for fear someone will find out where she came from, find out that the coat-of-arms has been painted over. What then? I don't want to hang, Elvira. I did it for the sake of our love. You know all that. We must move on.

(He comes to a stop)

Now you're crying again.

ELVIRA: That's just it, Pelegrin; you don't even see why things can't go on like this, not for me, not for a woman.

PELEGRIN: Why can't they go on?

ELVIRA: I wasn't born for this kind of life. I can't go on. It was a lovely dream by which I was seduced —

PELEGRIN: A dream.

ELVIRA: I feel that I'm waking up, and I can't go on any longer.

PELEGRIN: A dream. I understand. And reality is the castle that the other man has promised you, the nobleman. You left him. A dream. Now you remember that he promised you a castle. That's reality. I understand.

ELVIRA: What horrible things you can say!

PELEGRIN: God in heaven, what am I to do then? Tell me what you want me to do!

ELVIRA: I keep telling you all the time.

PELEGRIN: What?

ELVIRA: I want us to stay together.

PELEGRIN: What else do you think I want?

ELVIRA: For ever. Don't you understand that? I want us to stay in one place of which I can say: this is our home. That's all. One day we shall have a child, Pelegrin.

PELEGRIN: Yes.

ELVIRA: Can you grasp that?

PELEGRIN: A child?

ELVIRA: Can you grasp that?

PELEGRIN: Let it come, if it wants to. Let it see how wide the world is, how marvellous is man! What else?

ELVIRA: I should like us to marry, Pelegrin.

PELEGRIN: Marry...

(He breaks away from her)

I have feared that word. For a long time. And now, when the ship is seaworthy and the seas lie open to us again, at this moment when they are hoisting the sails, at this moment you utter it.

ELVIRA: I didn't ask you to abduct me, Pelegrin.

PELEGRIN: Marry!

ELVIRA: I only want what every woman who loves wants from the man she loves —

PELEGRIN: A nest, which we shall never leave again.

ELVIRA: If you don't know any nicer word for it, yes.

PELEGRIN: Call it a coffin, if you prefer. Marriage is a coffin for love... Just this: you want the man to cut off his wings, the little bits of wings a human being has. That's all you want from him.

ELVIRA: Men never think of anyone but themselves.

PELEGRIN: And you?

ELVIRA: I'm thinking of the child.

PELEGRIN: Always the child.

ELVIRA: Don't think the child is smaller than we. The life that lies before it is longer than ours.

PELEGRIN: Am I to bury myself for the child's sake? Must I kill myself so that it can live? *(He has to laugh)* Elvira! I can see the whole thing. I can see us living in a safe and settled place: I shall dig coal, so that we can live, or imagine we are living; or I shall deal in cod-liver oil. Why not! I shall earn big money, it will be my ambition to see that there is no cod-liver oil sold within a radius of a hundred miles that does not enrich me. As God is my witness, I shall improve cod-liver oil. For love of you! I shall not rest, day after day, week after week, year after year, so that we can live, live in security. Why do we live? Why — cod-liver oil demands it, duty, security for wife and child, for the chambermaid, the manservant, the cook, the labourer, God, the fatherland . . . *(With complete seriousness)* Elvira, I can't do that —

ELVIRA: It's a sacrifice, I know.

PELEGRIN: No one can do what he cannot want to do . . . and even you can't want that. I shall sit in the house for love of you, but my longing will be against you. Can you want that?

ELVIRA: Not I, Pelegrin —

PELEGRIN: Who then? Who else has a say in our love?

ELVIRA: The child —

PELEGRIN: Elvira, I can't marry. I can't do it.

PEDRO: *(Who is still sitting in the foreground)* They say the ship is seaworthy. There is a light west wind blowing over the bay.

(Pedro stays where he is)

ELVIRA: I shall travel no further, Pelegrin.

PELEGRIN: Elvira!

ELVIRA: You will leave me — if you sail.

PELEGRIN: Hasn't it been beautiful, all that we have experienced up till now? The shoreless nights out at sea, our nights, the silvery dancing of the waves, the glittering path of the moonlight, and all the rest of it to which no one can give a name; and then the mornings, the sunshine, the sails overhead, the blue skies, the stillness of the roaring wind, the foaming waves racing past: our day, our day without shores . . . do you regret all that, Elvira?

ELVIRA: I regret nothing.

PELEGRIN: God above, wasn't all that beautiful?

ELVIRA: It was — so long as I was a girl . . . Life is strange, Pelegrin, life goes forward unceasingly, it takes happiness away from us even while we hold it in our hands. I'm not a girl any more.

PELEGRIN: Oh, I beseech you —

ELVIRA: No one can do what he cannot want to do. How right you are!

PELEGRIN: Let's sail!

ELVIRA: You see, Pelegrin, I can't either.

(He remains silent)

Stay with me, Pelegrin. What is Hawaii? A name, a word.

PELEGRIN: You can't either . . .

ELVIRA: And suppose I ask you: darling, why do you want to go to Hawaii? What makes this island somewhere in the Pacific Ocean seem to you marvellous above all else? It is simply the fear of having to do without it. That is Hawaii.

PELEGRIN: You won't come with me . . .

ELVIRA: Stay with me, Pelegrin!

PELEGRIN: And I can't stay, and neither of us wants to leave the other, we love each other, and we cannot part without betraying our love, without becoming guilty, and if we stay together one of us will perish, one of us will be doing what he cannot do, cannot, and that too is a crime in the eyes of the other, that too . . .

(He falls to his knees)

What shall we do, God above, what shall we do, a man and a woman, whom God created for each other, that they should love each other, who must love each other — what are they to do that is not an absurdity?

(The Negro has reappeared, holds out his basket to Pelegrin)

NEGRO: Fresh oysters, gentlemen, fresh oysters.

PELEGRIN: Go to hell!

NEGRO: Absolutely fresh. You gentlemen can try them, if you don't believe me —

PELEGRIN: You can go to hell.

NEGRO: Not one of them is a corpse, on my honour, you gentlemen can poke them if you like and see for yourselves how they wriggle . . .

PELEGRIN: Go to hell, I said. They stink to high heaven.

NEGRO: Where do they stink to?

PELEGRIN: To high heaven!

NEGRO: Just now —

PELEGRIN: And you, for the last time, go to hell where you came from!

NEGRO: I'll tell you where I came from. Just now I was serving a foreign nobleman, a real nobleman, who had just landed, and he ate twenty oysters — corpses all of them, on my honour; now I've got nothing but lively little fellows, fresh as you like.

PELEGRIN: I say they stink.

(Suddenly a scuffle starts)

They stink, they stink . . .

NEGRO: Help! I'm being strangled! Help!

PELEGRIN: I say they stink.

(A crowd gathers)

THE CROWD: What's going on? What's happening? They're fighting! It's over. No, they're still at it! It's too late . . .

NEGRO: He tried to strangle me. I'll get the police. He must pay for all of them! I'm going for the police.

PELEGRIN: Come, Elvira, come.

(Pelegrin and Elvira leave, the Negro gets up, the crowd start trying the oysters, which are lying in the street. The Cavalry Captain appears in the jerkin of his youth. He looks around and sees Pedro, who is lying in the foreground)

PEDRO: . . . Quite right, Your Honour. This is the port of Santa Cruz. It seems Your Honour has just arrived?

CAPTAIN: A lively place.

PEDRO: Much ado about nothing.

CAPTAIN: I like a bit of life. *(Taking off his gloves)* Are you a soothsayer?

PEDRO: In a sense.

CAPTAIN: I thought so.

PEDRO: Your Honour is remarkably perspicacious — even in the hour of secret bewilderment: you see my irons and you know at once that I'm a soothsayer.

CAPTAIN: *(He laughs politely, but then stops as a thought strikes him)* In the hour of secret bewilderment? What do you mean by that?

PEDRO: Who knows better than you?

CAPTAIN: What?

PEDRO: Your Honour wishes to travel.

CAPTAIN: Any child could guess that, when it sees a man with luggage and in Santa Cruz. You don't have to be a soothsayer to know that! What else?

PEDRO: Yes, what else . . .

CAPTAIN: I wonder.

PEDRO: You know very well: a woman has left you . . . Perhaps it was many years ago, perhaps it was last night. That makes no difference. A woman you love has gone off with someone else. Maybe it will often happen again, exactly the same thing, and again and again you will stand at this spot: in front of you the open sea, the ships, the masts, the other life. You stand there with a pounding heart, distressed by a secret bewilderment, asking yourself: What now?

CAPTAIN: Yes, what now?

PEDRO: You are a nobleman.

CAPTAIN: What do you mean by that?

PEDRO: You can't take revenge on a woman in distress, for example. You can't be as selfish as you would like. You can't act like other people, whom you will envy all your life long.

CAPTAIN: Why can't I?

PEDRO: Because no one could have lived a different life from the one he has lived ... That is the truth I want to tell you: Even if you come back again to Santa Cruz — perhaps later, after many years have passed — with the intention of setting out on a journey, things will never be different from the way they are today. You can't act differently; you're a nobleman.

(For a while the Captain remains dumbfounded, then he tries to smile)

CAPTAIN: What does this wisdom cost?

PEDRO: Tears, secret tears and sleepless nights — nothing else.

(Pelegrin comes back out of the house, hurriedly, feverishly, determined)

PELEGRIN: Pedro —

CAPTAIN: God be with you.

PELEGRIN: With you too ... We're putting to sea, Pedro, at once.

CAPTAIN: May I ask where you're bound?

PELEGRIN: Hawaii.

(To Pedro)

We're putting to sea, I say. The Negro with his damn oysters has gone for the police. But we have to avoid the police. We have a coat-of-arms that has been painted over; we must move on.

PEDRO: I understand.

PELEGRIN: We must move on, I can't marry, I can't get myself hanged! *(To the Captain)* Sir, I wasn't polite just now —

CAPTAIN: Oh, you're in a hurry.

PELEGRIN: Hawaii ... Do you know what that means? What that is? What that stands for?

CAPTAIN: It's an island.

PELEGRIN: That too.

CAPTAIN: A very long way from here —

PELEGRIN: The further the better!

CAPTAIN: That's just how I feel.

PELEGRIN: Hawaii . . . Hawaii . . .

(As though it was the Captain, not Elvira, who said that Hawaii was nothing special)

You know, it's a place where lemons grow, pineapples, peaches, figs, dates, bananas, all of them together! I tell you, there is no winter there —

CAPTAIN: No winter.

PELEGRIN: Not a hint of winter, you know. I once knew a sailor who had been to Hawaii. He had a stick, an old Dutch thorn-stick. He left it standing in Hawaii. By mistake you understand. He had been leaning on the stick as he looked at a girl. You can imagine what I mean . . . perhaps you've heard about the girls of Hawaii? Anyhow, he went after one of those girls and left the stick standing. A year later, as the fate of a sailor would have it, he came back to Hawaii . . . What do you think had happened? The stick he left standing there by mistake, the old Dutch thorn-stick, was in flower —

CAPTAIN: In flower?

PELEGRIN: That's Hawaii.

CAPTAIN: And that's where you're bound?

PELEGRIN: Are you going to tell me, Hawaii is nothing special?

(He shakes hands with the Captain)

Good bye!

CAPTAIN: There's something I want to ask you...

PELEGRIN: My name? I have no name.

CAPTAIN: Will you take me with you? If I pay?

PELEGRIN: Because of the thorn-stick?

CAPTAIN: Will you take me with you?

PELEGRIN: My dear sir — are you serious?

CAPTAIN: It's the longing of a man who has no other longing left.

PELEGRIN: I see...

CAPTAIN: You hesitate.

PELEGRIN: It's a long way, you know —

CAPTAIN: It is better to travel than to arrive.

PELEGRIN: A pretty saying, very pretty; but the French may nab us. They're funny people, the French; they're looking for a ship, a particular ship that sank off the coast of Morocco, no one knows how... and then, you know, there are the storms, we have to sail round the Cape. Thirst, the monsoons, fever... fever, pirates —

CAPTAIN: I consider myself a man.

PELEGRIN: All right, if you pay — done!

(They shake hands)

We sail in a quarter of an hour. It's the ship with the red pennant.

(Going)

We sail in a quarter of an hour, my friend, we shan't wait —

(As a salutation) Hawaii!

CAPTAIN: Hawaii!

(Pelegrin leaves, from the other side comes the crowd, with the Negro and the Policeman in the middle)

NEGRO: This is where he strangled me.

POLICEMAN: So you say.

NEGRO: And here, I swear, he threw my oysters into the street.

POLICEMAN: There's no sign of that either.

NEGRO: Even a Negro deserves to be believed!

POLICEMAN: We'll leave racism out of it . . . We'll go into the house he fled into.

(They enter the house, leaving the Captain and Kilian, the Servant, looking as he might have looked seventeen years ago)

SERVANT: This too?

CAPTAIN: Everything, I tell you. It has to be down below in a quarter of an hour.

SERVANT: In a quarter of an hour?

CAPTAIN: Have you got that straight, Kilian: it's the ship with the red pennant.

SERVANT: That rust bucket, Your Honour?

(He drags the luggage together)

Your Honour, I can't stand the sea. In pictures, yes. It's such a lovely colour, but it generally stinks . . . I imagined it all differently, Your Honour. I thought I was going to be a servant at the castle. That's what it says in our contract. I thought I would put the glasses on the table, draw the curtains, bring the candles, put the wood in the fireplace —

CAPTAIN: Forward, Kilian, forward!

SERVANT: In the garden too, Your Honour, I could have helped in the garden too. When I think of how well I could have done as a servant in a castle!

CAPTAIN: My good fellow, I imagined things differently too.

SERVANT: Such a fine castle we could have had, Your Honour.

(He picks up the things)

The ship with the dirty pennant, you said?

(The Policeman and the Negro come out of the house)

NEGRO: We've got her!

POLICEMAN: I'm sorry, lovely lady, that your beau is such a scoundrel that he runs off and would rather leave his girl in the lurch than pay for the oysters. I'm sorry . . .

NEGRO: Even a Negro should be believed, lady.

(To the policeman:)

He said they stink, they stink, they stink —

(The Captain catches sight of Elvira who has appeared in the doorway)

CAPTAIN: You, Elvira!

NEGRO: Ei, ei! Ei, ei!

POLICEMAN: Hold your white tongue!

CAPTAIN: Officer —

POLICEMAN: Your Honour?

CAPTAIN: What happened here?

NEGRO: I'm a Negro —

POLICEMAN: Nothing special, Your Honour, this sort of thing happens every day.

NEGRO: I'm a Negro —

POLICEMAN: You don't have to keep saying what everyone can see for himself. He's a poor fellow, someone tried to choke him, but they didn't succeed.

NEGRO: This gentleman bought some of my oysters himself and I ask the gentleman: How were my oysters, were they fresh or not?

POLICEMAN: Your Honour, that has nothing to do with it. His oysters were thrown into the street, fact. Someone has to pay for them, fact. The fact that he's a Negro has nothing to do with it either.

CAPTAIN: I'll pay for them.

POLICEMAN: That's not necessary, Your Honour, we have a fund that will cover it —

CAPTAIN: And leave the girl in peace.

(The Captain pays)

NEGRO: A crafty gentleman.

POLICEMAN: Where are your manners?

NEGRO: Sir, I didn't throw the oysters into the street.

(Grinning)

A crafty gentleman: He pays for the oysters and buys the girl.

(The Captain and Elvira remain alone)

CAPTAIN: So we meet again here.

ELVIRA: Yes, it's sad.

CAPTAIN: As you can see, Elvira, I'm going on a journey.

ELVIRA: Where to?

CAPTAIN: Hawaii...

ELVIRA: I scarcely dared to hope that we would ever meet again. And yet I always pictured the way it was bound to be. And I was desperately ashamed, although none of it was my fault; nevertheless I was ashamed.

CAPTAIN: The woman is never to blame, I know. The mere fact that it looks as though the woman doesn't act speaks in her favour.

ELVIRA: How well I understand your bitter words! How sorry I am for you that you should see me like this...

CAPTAIN: Thank you for your sympathy.

ELVIRA: You didn't deserve all that, my faithful friend!

CAPTAIN: Nevertheless I shall go on a journey.

ELVIRA: I can't stop you, I know, not with all my love. How could you believe in my love? I have never forgotten you...

(She hides her face)

It's all so horrible!

CAPTAIN: Elvira, I can't help it.

ELVIRA: My friend, how beautiful things could have been for us! When my father used to tell me about your castle, it always made me quite melancholy. What have I done to deserve that? I used to say. What have I done to deserve to live in a castle? Then my father would laugh and say: It's because you're beautiful, Elvira... And that is exactly what brought about my downfall, that is what smashed in pieces all that we might both have had, that is why I am stuck in this place and can be grateful for the generosity that bought my freedom from the Negro.

CAPTAIN: You mustn't talk like that.

ELVIRA: Grateful for the anguished sorrow, my friend, of having been permitted to see you once again. I wouldn't sacrifice my anguish, even to make all this never have happened.

(The Servant fetches the last piece of luggage)

SERVANT: Your Honour, they're weighing anchor . . .

(The servant leaves with the last piece of luggage)

ELVIRA: I shall understand if you abandon me now. After all that has happened I shall understand completely.

CAPTAIN: And you?

ELVIRA: You have a perfect right to do so. I have no right to be angry if you abandon me . . .

CAPTAIN: And you?

ELVIRA: Don't worry about me.

CAPTAIN: Elvira!

ELVIRA: Your servant said they're weighing anchor . . .

CAPTAIN: Tell me, what will become of you?

ELVIRA: I tell you: Farewell!

CAPTAIN: And you? What about you? Tell me that.

ELVIRA: They're weighing anchor. Do you hear? It is as though I could feel it in my own body: they weigh anchor, then they push off with the long poles, then they put the wheel over, it creaks, then the sails fill with wind . . . My head is reeling. I don't want to stay and then regret having stayed; I don't want you to stay with me out of pity, out of decency . . . What is to become of me? I shall wait for you. Perhaps for you to come back again; what else could I do with my love for you but wait for you, but gaze after you, after your pennant as it sinks below the horizon of this hour, and yet hope, and yet love you! . . .

CAPTAIN: Who are you talking about?

ELVIRA: Who am I talking about? About you . . .

(She collapses, so that he has to hold her)

SERVANT: Your Honour?

CAPTAIN: Silence!

SERVANT: Your Honour, they're putting to sea . . .

CAPTAIN: I know.

(They stand motionless — while Pedro, the only one still moving, comes to the front of the stage. He is no longer in irons and dangles the irons in his hand)

PEDRO: That's more or less how it was then, more or less like that . . . They went to the castle of their marriage, Elvira and the Captain. He's a nobleman, I've already said that. He can't act differently. A child was born. The Other Man sailed round the Cape; in Madagascar the French caught him. The prospect of the galleys, his fever, how a nurse gave him blood — we know all about that already . . . We will just act the last scene: today, seventeen years later. This, as we also know, is the last night Pelegrin has to live.

ACT 5

In the castle. Pelegrin is standing at the window, as we saw him in the scene before last. He is still cracking nuts. Elvira is sitting in an armchair, waiting; the candles are alight.

PELEGRIN: In an hour dawn will break.

ELVIRA: I ask you again, Pelegrin: what did you tell the Captain? You drank together till midnight, I hear —

PELEGRIN: Drank?

ELVIRA: Did you tell the Captain what happened between us at that time? Seventeen years ago. The way men talk among themselves?

PELEGRIN: The way men talk among themselves. How would you know that? You mustn't believe everything you read in books, Elvira.

ELVIRA: I implore you, Pelegrin: what did you tell him?

PELEGRIN: About us, you mean?

ELVIRA: About us.

PELEGRIN: Not a word.

ELVIRA: Not a word?

PELEGRIN: I had no idea the Captain knew nothing about it. To tell you the truth, I never thought for a moment of all the harm I could have done . . .

(Reaches into his pocket)

Wonderful nuts you have.

ELVIRA: I don't know what to think. About last night. What did happen?

PELEGRIN: I told him about Hawaii —

ELVIRA: Hawaii?

(Servant enters)

ELVIRA: And?

PELEGRIN: He didn't say much himself.

ELVIRA: And?

SERVANT: My Lady, we went to the stable. As Your Ladyship ordered.

ELVIRA: Well?

SERVANT: Two horses have gone, Rosinante and Casanova. And the sleigh has gone too.

ELVIRA: It's not a dream.

SERVANT: Your Ladyship, the Captain has set out on a journey.

ELVIRA: On a journey . . . ?

SERVANT: As I told you before.

ELVIRA: In the middle of the night? Out into the snow?

SERVANT: It seems so, My Lady.

ELVIRA: What madness . . . Who harnessed the horses for him, I should like to know! In the middle of the night! Wake the servants, question them. And send the idiot here.

SERVANT: Whatever you like to call him, My Lady, it was me.

ELVIRA: You yourself?

SERVANT: The master ordered me to.

ELVIRA: And then, when every second counts if we are to catch up with him, then you go out to the stable to see if the sleigh which you harnessed yourself is still there!

SERVANT: Your Ladyship ordered me to.

ELVIRA: God above, what's the meaning of all this — ?

SERVANT: Your Ladyship wouldn't believe me.

ELVIRA: On a journey, you say? Where to?

SERVANT: The master didn't say where he was going.

ELVIRA: What did he say then?

SERVANT: The master said, for example —

ELVIRA: Make sure you tell me exactly!

SERVANT: Quietly! he said. Our mistress is asleep, our mistress is dreaming —

ELVIRA: Dreaming?

SERVANT: Quietly! he said, so that our mistress shall not wake up; I think her dream is beautiful!

ELVIRA: What else did he say?

SERVANT: Kilian, he said, hold my coat for me —

ELVIRA: What else?

SERVANT: Kilian, you have never understood life, he said. Life is a joyful thing, life is a great dream.

ELVIRA: What else?

SERVANT: That was all, that's exactly what he said.

(A brief silence)

ELVIRA: Let someone mount the other horse, my own horse. At once! Let him ride after the Captain until he finds out what all this means. And even if my horse falls dead, I shall reward him so handsomely that his grandchildren will still talk about it.

SERVANT: As Your Ladyship orders.

ELVIRA: I shall wait here.

(The servant goes)

My good husband, my dear husband! God grant nothing happens to him!

PELEGRIN: In an hour dawn will break.

ELVIRA: He has gone riding out into the snow, into this flood of snow; only three days ago they planted the saplings, all along the road; by yesterday there was not a twig to be seen, nothing, nothing! When I think of him driving through this blizzard — what madness!

(Turning to Pelegrin)

Why are you doing all this to us?

(Pelegrin looks round)

Yes — you!

PELEGRIN: What am I doing to you?

ELVIRA: Why did you come here? What do you want?

PELEGRIN: I was invited.

ELVIRA: I tell you, Pelegrin, our marriage is happy, perfectly happy, however much people may smile about marriage —

PELEGRIN: Who does that?

ELVIRA: There's something wonderful about marriage! When we married, seventeen years ago, I didn't know how much, how honestly, I should one day be able to love him! People have to get to know each other, the way we did, without being in love. A man like him, I almost didn't deserve him. *(Smiling)* Sometimes, when I can't see him, he seems to me like God himself, you can rely upon him so completely. Last year, after I had been ill with flu for ten weeks, when I was allowed up for the first time — I suddenly remembered my parrot. I must have forgotten all about him. But he was alive! My husband had fed him, for ten weeks, although he loathes him. That's how he is, he thinks of everything . . .

(Pelegrin chews nuts and nods)

That's the awful thing; whatever he does, I know quite well he is doing it for my sake. And if he goes out into the night and leaves me, the whole madness of this sudden departure — perhaps he thinks I want to be alone with you. The good man! He doesn't know that you mean absolutely nothing to me any more . . . Kilian . . .

(The servant has reappeared)

What is it?

SERVANT: Your Ladyship —

ELVIRA: Has he come back? God grant that he has!

SERVANT: Your Ladyship, I've brought fresh candles.

(He puts them down and leaves)

PELEGRIN: You were asking what I want.

(He comes back from the window)

I was sitting in the inn — yes, it's a week ago already — I heard who lived in this castle, a coincidence! A different coincidence and I should never have heard about it: we should never have met again on this earth. A hundred paces and we should have gone past each other, you and I, out into the night . . .

(Elvira remains silent)

Tomorrow I shall travel on.

(Elvira remains silent)

It seemed to me so wonderful that two people could be in the same place at the same time, that they could live on this earth at the same time . . . just that, nothing more . . . I took the guitar, I don't know what else I wanted; I wanted music.

ELVIRA: Didn't you say you wanted to pay me a visit?

PELEGRIN: Yes, you could put it like that.

ELVIRA: Why? *(Scornfully)* Because we loved each other, long ago?

PELEGRIN: Yes, I believe that too, I believe that we once loved each other.

ELVIRA: And since you happened to be in the neighbourhood you felt like coming to see how much of it was left? Oh, I understand.

(Pelegrin looks at her and says nothing)

Or you wanted to find out in passing whether Elvira knew how far you had got — without her. Round the world. I know all about it, my chambermaid told me, full of admiration.

(Pelegrin looks at her and says nothing)

Or perhaps you wanted to find out whether I'm happy, even though you behaved like a scoundrel towards me — seventeen years ago.

PELEGRIN: That's what you say.

ELVIRA: Yes, I am happy, Pelegrin. I am. What more do you want? Shall I make a signed statement, so that you can go away from here reassured?

PELEGRIN: I should have believed it without your signature, without your offer of a signature.

ELVIRA: Once, years ago, you wrote to me; you sent me greetings from Java, I believe.

PELEGRIN: Korea.

ELVIRA: Do you know how I felt as I held those silly greetings in my hand, that silly chit-chat after so many years?

PELEGRIN: If we knew how the receiver felt, Elvira, who would ever write another letter? That's the magic of a letter: it's an act of audacity . . .

ELVIRA: I shuddered with shame to think that I had once loved with all my heart the fellow who had written that rubbish. Yes, I felt disgusted by you! Do you understand that?

PELEGRIN: To tell you the truth, no . . . No, actually I don't.

ELVIRA: The older our marriage grew in this house, the more disgusted I felt by such a coward as you are. You wished me, as you wrote on that silly scrap of paper, a faithful and trustworthy husband . . .

PELEGRIN: I meant it quite seriously.

ELVIRA: Yes, so that you could withdraw into the realm of the lost, where people remain young and immortal, indestructible! That's how it was. You didn't want marriage so that my longing for you should be kept alive. It was unbelievably cunning. You wanted more than a wife beside you; you wanted to be in her dreams! And you were quite prepared to leave reality, the nearby and the everyday, that is used up and made empty by the thousand kisses of habit, to the other man, the faithful and trustworthy husband you had wished me ... Why? So that I should have no other lover, bound as I was by marital fidelity, no other but the lover from the past — no other but you! *(Pelegrin smiles)* Isn't that how it was?

PELEGRIN: I must admit that I have never thought about it that much.

ELVIRA: Think about it, and in the end you will find a scoundrel, a murderer of love, a coward in the face of real life, which you never had the courage to use to the full, never, not with the other women either because I know I wasn't the only one ...

PELEGRIN: Elvira!

ELVIRA: Will you contradict that?

PELEGRIN: Naturally you weren't the only one, Elvira, my dear Elvira, that goes without saying.

ELVIRA: I understand.

PELEGRIN: Perhaps you are the only one who does understand that ...

ELVIRA: I understand men's infidelity; it's a form of self-flattery, the equivalent of our showy dresses, no more; you try to give yourselves the glitter of adventure, of passion at any price, to satisfy your vanity ...

(In an emotional outburst)

Pelegrin, why did you come? I don't understand at all, not at all! Tell me why. After seventeen years! What do you want with me?

(He says nothing)

Did you come here to crack nuts? To leaf through a book?

PELEGRIN: Why not?

ELVIRA: Why not ...

PELEGRIN: I love the books I don't know.

ELVIRA: Did you come to see whether I was still attached to you? Yearning for you? Waiting for you?

(He leafs through a book)

Or did you want to see how I hate you, how I see through you, how I despise you?

(He leafs through the book)

Why did you come? To make the past touch us once more, that was all you wanted; mutual forgiveness, all in a romantic vein, we would smile, we would joke about the tears we had shed, nothing more; revive the memory of an episode, and nostalgia would make another little episode out of it, an echo of past bliss, a passing visit, a sentimental evening over nuts and wine . . .

(He leafs through the book)

You say nothing.

PELEGRIN: Elvira, you're not being generous . . . You're trying to force me to speak. To lie. To explain myself. All you want is to hear from my mouth the word that will put me in the wrong — so that you shall be free of me . . . I don't know, Elvira, why you're afraid of your own heart.

ELVIRA: Am I afraid?

PELEGRIN: Does anyone know how it was then? All those years ago. Do you or I know what the whole truth is now, as we wait here in the night?

(He takes another book)

If we could only have kept silent for an hour, as we stand here! Just that . . . You could have embroidered or read; I should have looked at these books, butterflies, all these painted plants — *Melaleuca folia*, for example . . . and then, yes, then I should have moved on.

ELVIRA: And then?

PELEGRIN: For ever, I think.

ELVIRA: And then?

PELEGRIN: Life would have been all around us again.

(He sits down at the clavichord)

In Honolulu I met a ship's captain who was getting on in years and now had only one love, astronomy. Nothing was more important to him. We used to laugh at him, because that was all he could talk about. Everything else had become insignificant, since he found a big thick book in his cabin. Maybe it was the first book he had read in his life. And he read it every minute of the day! When he came into the tavern where we were dancing with the negro girls, he would tell us about the Milky Way, as though it had come into being yesterday . . .

(He takes an orange from the bowl)

Whenever we sat down with him he would take an orange like this and say: This is the moon. He got annoyed if anyone smiled. And that globe there, that's the earth. And that's the moon. They had to be seven paces apart, I still remember that clearly. And what's in between? he asked. Not even air, not even light, nothing but night, the void, death, nothing that deserves to be given a name — nothing!

ELVIRA: Who said that?

PELEGRIN: The ship's captain in Honolulu . . . Let's suppose I have a sister who stayed behind in Europe, and let's suppose she is standing in the market in Barcelona, and she's holding a melon in her hands: that's the first star, a melon in Barcelona. And what is there between that star and the next? Nothing but night, the void, death. That's how big nothingness is, my friends, that's how little there is of life, of warmth, of what exists, of what you understand, the little bit of light flickering in the dark. So little of what exists.

(He peels the orange)

I wouldn't bet one slice that the interrelationships are correct. He was a rum customer. After that, I couldn't peel an orange without thinking of all that.

ELVIRA: Why are you telling me this?

PELEGRIN: It just came into my head . . . If we had peeled an orange together, Elvira, life would have been around us again.

(She listens)

ELVIRA: Wasn't that a sleigh-bell?

(It seems not to have been)

PELEGRIN: Listening to you as you spoke tonight, I heard only how clever you are.

ELVIRA: And women aren't supposed to be clever!

PELEGRIN: I believe you have secrets which your intelligence has to protect; you need your intelligence very badly, that's why it's so acute.

ELVIRA: Have you come to tell me your own secrets?

PELEGRIN: What do they matter to me?

ELVIRA: That's just it, you don't want to know why you came!

PELEGRIN: Could it really not be, Elvira, that I wanted nothing more at all?

ELVIRA: And yet you came.

PELEGRIN: And yet I came.

(He eats his orange)

I thought it would be right, in fact beautiful. We're not judges over one another, I thought to myself. You may consider me a scoundrel; God will receive me as such, if I was; and for my part I think at this moment that women are not magnanimous. God, if he thinks the same, will receive you accordingly . . . But in any case, I thought, we met each other in this life, we loved each other, each in our own way, each in keeping with our age, each in keeping with our sex. And both of us are still living: now at this moment, in this place. Why shouldn't we say hello to each other? I thought to myself.

ELVIRA: Why should we?

PELEGRIN: Our life is short.

ELVIRA: Did you by any chance think you could abduct me again?

PELEGRIN: What for?

ELVIRA: One more episode for a man . . .

(Pelegrin plays one or two notes on the clavichord. In the manner of a child who would like to play, but has never learned. Viola has already appeared, she is standing in the doorway in her nightgown)

ELVIRA: In God's name, child . . . ! What are you doing here?

VIOLA: I can't sleep.

ELVIRA: At this time of night!

VIOLA: I'm so terribly afraid, Mama . . .

ELVIRA: What of?

VIOLA: I'm having such dreadful dreams, Mama . . .

ELVIRA: But child!

VIOLA: Mama, there's death in the house.

(She looks at her mother, then takes fright at her own certainty, she is weeping, Elvira has to hold her)

ELVIRA: Come Viola, come. Sit down. Don't be afraid! It was just a dream that scared you. That's all. Don't cry. We'll have a cup of tea . . . do you hear? I'll fetch your coat . . . Kilian!

(Elvira goes out. Pelegrin tries to play the clavichord)

PELEGRIN: Dawn is breaking.

(Viola says nothing)

You mustn't be afraid, my dear child, not in the least. There's nothing dreadful about it; I've lived.

(Viola says nothing)

Can you play? If I had my life over again, I'd like to learn. It must be wonderful.

VIOLA: Oh yes!

PELEGRIN: Painting is wonderful too.

VIOLA: Oh yes, and lots of other things.

PELEGRIN: Lots and lots.

(Viola says nothing)

I know a seashell that doesn't exist, a shell that is so beautiful you can only imagine it, and even if you wandered along all the beaches in the world and opened a thousand seashells, all of them together wouldn't be as beautiful as the shell I can only imagine . . . But you are! That's what I used to say to the girls I loved. God knows I really meant it, and the girls believed me, just as I believed it myself. But girls fade away, they become women, and the women too fade away

— and in the end there's nothing left but the seashell that doesn't exist, the shell you can only imagine.

(The sound of sleigh bells)

May I ask, child, how old you are?

VIOLA: Me? Seventeen.

PELEGRIN: Seventeen.

VIOLA: Why are you looking at me like that?

(The sound of sleigh bells)

PELEGRIN: That's him, I think. There he is!

VIOLA: Who?

PELEGRIN: The Cavalry Captain: your father . . . We've known each other for seventeen years, your father and I. Even then he wanted to go to Hawaii, then like now.

VIOLA: My father?

PELEGRIN: He's a nobleman.

VIOLA: Then why didn't he go?

PELEGRIN: Because there was a child waiting for him, then as now . . . There he is, I think, go and meet him. There he is.

(Viola does as Pelegrin tells her, she slowly leaves, without taking her eyes off the stranger; he too keeps his eyes on her until she disappears into the darkness of the doorway)

PELEGRIN: You can't have both it seems. One has the sea, the other a castle; one has Hawaii — the other a child . . .

(Elvira comes back with the Secretary)

ELVIRA: What letter? Give it to me!

SECRETARY: Your Ladyship —

ELVIRA: Were you the one who rode after him?

SECRETARY: Your Ladyship, forgive my appearance. I've just got out of bed. It's the second time tonight I've been woken up . . .

ELVIRA: What letter is this?

SECRETARY: Our master, the Captain, wrote it during the night and told me to deliver it at breakfast.

ELVIRA: At breakfast?

SECRETARY: Kilian thought now, since Your Ladyship is already up . . .

(Elvira reads the letter)

Weren't those footsteps? Your Ladyship, I believe the Captain has come back . . .

(The Secretary, receiving no answer, leaves)

ELVIRA: So that's it! . . . He would like to live again, he writes, to be able to weep again, to be able to love and to thrill at the perfume of a night, to be able to exult: before the snow buries us to all eternity . . . Why couldn't we have been more honest?

(She can't see his face, as he sits at the clavichord; he is motionless and as pale as a wax mask)

Oh, Pelegrin! Don't believe a word I said to you tonight . . . I called you a scoundrel because I thought I was a scoundrel for having dreamt of you for seventeen years . . . Now I can say it, Pelegrin; it is good that you have come . . .

(The Captain is standing in the doorway)

ELVIRA: Why couldn't we have been more honest?

CAPTAIN: I wanted to go away.

ELVIRA: I know.

CAPTAIN: It isn't possible . . . What about you?

ELVIRA: I waited for you. I dreamed . . .

CAPTAIN: I know.

ELVIRA: And when I woke up I looked for you in vain through the whole house. I found Pelegrin here. I poured scorn on him, for your sake.

CAPTAIN: For my sake?

ELVIRA: For the sake of fidelity. For seventeen years I have thought I had to lie, I had to lie in order to be faithful to you, as I thought you were faithful to me . . . And then I read your letter, just this moment.

CAPTAIN: So you did.

ELVIRA: Why couldn't we have been more honest? We were so close to it. How we would have understood each other! You buried your longing, as you write, for years on end, so that I shouldn't be frightened; and I was ashamed of my dreams, for years on end, because I knew they would frighten you. Neither of us wanted to disappoint the other . . . that is the little comedy that we have been acting for so long — till Pelegrin came.

(She screams, becoming aware that Pelegrin is dead)

Pelegrin?

CAPTAIN: Now I understand . . .

ELVIRA: Why are you smiling like that?

CAPTAIN: Now I understand what he said to me last night. He said it so cheerfully I couldn't believe he meant it seriously.

ELVIRA: Pelegrin!

CAPTAIN: He knew.

ELVIRA: Why didn't you tell me, dear friend? Don't smile like that, I kneel before you. We have done one another wrong, all of us. God meant all that to be far more beautiful . . . We can love one another, all of us, now I can see that: life is different, love is greater, fidelity is deeper, it has no need to fear our dreams; we have no need to kill our longing, no need to lie . . . Oh Pelegrin! Can you hear me? Can you hear me? We will eat an orange together. Life will be around us once again . . . Don't smile like that!

CAPTAIN: Elvira . . .

ELVIRA: Why didn't I hear it while you were still speaking, why?

CAPTAIN: Don't cry, Elvira. There is nothing terrible about it. He said: I regret nothing I have experienced, there is nothing I wish to repeat . . . He said it so cheerfully.

(Fade into darkness)

(As all the surroundings fade into darkness — the walls of the room and Elvira and the Captain who has to hold her as she swoons, as he held her once before, when Pelegrin left her — music rings out and the figures appear from all sides)

THE FIRST FIGURE: I bring the first coffee from Cuba.

THE SECOND FIGURE: I am the girl you never touched, Anatolia.

THE THIRD FIGURE: I bring you the fruits: pineapples, peaches, figs, grapes. They are next year's fruits, the fruits of the year to come.

THE FOURTH FIGURE: I am the nurse who gave you blood, in the hospital on Madagascar.

THE FIFTH FIGURE: I bring you the books: Sophocles, Virgil, Confucius, Byron, Cervantes and everything you would have wanted to read again. Honeycombs filled with the spirit of the centuries, spattered with candle wax.

THE SIXTH FIGURE: I am the skipper from Honolulu, who, God knows why, will have to remember you three more times.

THE SEVENTH FIGURE: I bring you the wine you have spilled.

THE EIGHTH FIGURE: I am the mother you never saw, Pelegrin; I died of you.

THE NINTH FIGURE: I am death.

PELEGRIN: We know that . . .

THE LAST FIGURE: I am the child of your blood, Viola, who will learn everything afresh, who will begin all over again.

NOW THEY'RE SINGING AGAIN

Attempt at a Requiem

The locale of the following events is always clear from the spoken word. Scenery should be used only insofar as it is required by the actors, and in no case should it attempt to create an illusion of reality. For the fact that we are watching a play must be constantly evident, lest anyone be tempted to compare these scenes with the real events, which were monstrous. We did not even witness them with our own eyes, and we must ask ourselves whether we have any right to speak at all. The only possible justification for speaking is the fact that we, who did not suffer in person, are free from all temptation to vengeance. Nevertheless the doubt remains. There are certain scenes which those who grieve from a distance cannot help picturing, even if only under the involuntary compulsion of dreams, such as torment all those who live today. Different people will picture different scenes.

CHARACTERS

Herbert • Karl • Parish Priest of the Orthodox Church • Maria • Senior Teacher • Liesel • Flying-Officer • The Other • Edward • Radio Operator • Benjamin • Flight-Lieutenant • Leading Aircraftman • Thomas • The Woman • Someone • Block Warden • Air-Raid Warden • The Old Man • The Child • Jenny • The Boy • Soldier

PART ONE
___

SCENE 1

Herbert, an officer, and Karl, a private.

HERBERT: In an hour it will be night . . . We must get out of here; our task is done.

KARL: Yes, in an hour it will be night . . .

HERBERT: What's the matter with you?

KARL: Our task is done . . .

HERBERT: You're looking at the world as though you had shot yourself!

KARL: We must get out of here . . .

HERBERT: As soon as the priest has finished, as soon as he has filled in the grave.

KARL: Our task is done . . .

HERBERT: That's the third time you've said that!

KARL: In the spring, when the snow melts, in the spring I shall have leave . . . in the spring, when the buds come, when the sun comes, then this trench will also appear. We can order the priest: Dig a grave of such and such a length and be quick about it! We can order him:

NOW THEY'RE SINGING AGAIN

Now fill the grave in again and be quick about it! We can give orders to everything in this world, everything, except to the grass that is to grow over the grave, and be quick about it. People will see the trench of such and such a length . . . in the spring, when the snow melts, in the spring, when I am home on leave with Mother, eating cake.

HERBERT: Have a cigarette!

(Herbert gives him a cigarette)

KARL: Yeast cake . . . Thank you . . . They've been saving up flour and sugar for a whole year for that yeast cake!

(Herbert gives him a light)

At one time, when I was a boy, I liked yeast cake more than anything . . .

HERBERT: Smoke your cigarette and stop blathering; you're tired, Karl.

KARL: In spring I shall have leave.

HERBERT: We can do anything, except get tired, except lose our nerve, that's something we mustn't do, Karl, never.

KARL: In an hour it will be night . . . Maria writes that she can hear the swallows. At this time of year! She can see the butterflies! At this time of year! Maria writes that the brooks are waiting for us to come home on leave, waiting under the snow . . .

> *Spring's blue ribbon now is streaming*
> *Once more through the balmy air.*

Do you know Mörike?

HERBERT: Perhaps better than you.

KARL: I love him.

NOW THEY'RE SINGING AGAIN

HERBERT: *Sweet, familiar scents are teeming*
Round us full of promise rare.
Violets already dreaming
In a hurry to appear.
Hark, far-off a gentle harpstring
Spring it is you.
It is your voice I hear.

(Silence)

KARL: Herbert, can you tell me why we shot those twenty-one people?

HERBERT: What does it matter to you?

KARL: I shot them —

HERBERT: They were hostages.

KARL: They sang. Did you hear how they sang?

HERBERT: Now they're silent.

KARL: They sang — to the last.

(Herbert looks across)

HERBERT: I can see it coming: the old priest will make a legend of it, if we let him talk, if we let him live.

KARL: Herbert!

HERBERT: What is it?

KARL: Does that mean that the priest too —

HERBERT: He's shovelling the earth as if he had planted a bulb, he's shovelling so carefully, and what a precious bulb; in spring, if all goes well, a tulip will rise from it!

KARL: Herbert, the priest has done no wrong —

HERBERT: Did we ask the hostages what wrong they had done? He's covering them over as though he really believed in their resurrection; now he's picking out the stones, one at a time!

KARL: Herbert, the priest has done no wrong —

(Herbert turns back again)

HERBERT: Did you notice that beautiful fresco? In the middle apse?

KARL: What fresco?

HERBERT: A Crucifixion and a Resurrection, what else? A remarkable thing, Byzantine, twelfth century perhaps, in excellent condition . . . I can't help thinking of your father, Karl.

KARL: Why?

HERBERT: Our teacher would lick his lips, if he could see them. And he would deliver a lecture: All these figures, he would say, are not portrayed against the background of a landscape, out of which they were born and which conditions them; they are portrayed against a background of gold, that is to say against the limitless space of the mind — and so on . . .

KARL: Why do you say that now, just now of all times?

HERBERT: I often think of our teacher, I can't look at anything without knowing what he with his culture would have to say about it. Anything beautiful, I mean. He never spoke about anything but the beautiful . . . Do you know how he is nowadays, by the way?

(The Priest has appeared)

Well, Little Father?

PRIEST: They are buried.

HERBERT: What about you?

PRIEST: I have buried them as you ordered.

HERBERT: An obedient man!

PRIEST: God give them rest.

HERBERT: What about you?

PRIEST: I don't understand it.

HERBERT: What?

PRIEST: Why God sent you.

HERBERT: So you believe God sent us?

(Herbert goes up to him)

Swear that you won't talk when we've gone; swear to that.

PRIEST: I swear.

HERBERT: Swear that you saw nothing with your own eyes.

PRIEST: You blindfolded me.

HERBERT: Swear to that!

PRIEST: I saw nothing, I swear.

HERBERT: And you heard nothing either?

PRIEST: They sang.

HERBERT: Swear that you heard nothing, or we'll shoot you too.

PRIEST: Me?

HERBERT: I shall count to ten. Do you understand?

PRIEST: Me?

HERBERT: One, two, three, four, five, six, seven —

PRIEST: I swear.

(The Priest is allowed to go)

HERBERT: They nauseate me, nauseate me, all these godly scoundrels!

KARL: If he had never met us, Herbert, he wouldn't have become a scoundrel; you made him one —

HERBERT: They're afraid, afraid, everyone's afraid of us!

KARL: That's the power we have.

HERBERT: And the spirit, which is supposed to be higher than our power, where is that? What else are we looking for but that? Where is he, that God whom they have been painting on all the walls for centuries, whose name is always on their lips? I don't hear him.

KARL: An hour ago they were singing —

HERBERT: Afraid, afraid, they're all afraid of our power; they swear oaths that are false, they are astonished that this God doesn't subdue us! We resorted to force, to the ultimate degree of violence, so that we should come face to face with the spirit. Let me find out if it is true what they say — let me see a single resurrection! I have shot hundreds, and I have seen no resurrection.

KARL: We have simply become murderers —

HERBERT: We resorted to force, to the ultimate degree of violence, so that we might come face to face with the spirit, the real spirit; but the scoffers are right, there is no real spirit, and we have the world in our pocket, whether we want it or not, I see no limit to our power — that brings despair.

(He turns around)

The priest will be shot.

KARL: Why?

HERBERT: Because I order it. I said: Dig a grave for these twenty-one people. He did it. I said: Fill it in again. He did it. I said: Swear by God that you heard nothing. He swore. Now I say: The priest will be shot . . .

KARL: I don't understand that . . .

HERBERT: And you, who don't understand it, you will do it.

KARL: I?

HERBERT: I order you to.

KARL: Herbert —

HERBERT: In five minutes it will be done.

(Karl stands in silence)

We can't believe his oath. He swears by a God who doesn't exist; if God existed he couldn't swear a false oath and go on his way. He will take revenge for his own treachery, as soon as he is no longer facing our gun barrels, be sure of that! Because he is afraid of us, and it is always fear, fear more than anything, that makes them think of revenge. I tell you, in five minutes he will be shot —

KARL: And suppose I tell you I won't do it?

HERBERT: You know what that means.

KARL: I know.

HERBERT: You wouldn't be the first.

KARL: I know.

HERBERT: I shall put you against the wall myself, if necessary, and straight away; you can believe me, Karl. We have always done what we said we would do; that is something not everyone can say of himself these days. We can be relied on.

NOW THEY'RE SINGING AGAIN

KARL: I know you.

HERBERT: Think it over.

KARL: And suppose I sing as you do it?

HERBERT: I'll give you five minutes.

KARL: And suppose I sing as you do it?

HERBERT: Afterwards there will be no more words. I'll give you five minutes.

(Herbert leaves)

KARL: Now they're singing again . . .

(The Priest appears and waits; the singing is heard)

PRIEST: I was told to report to you.

KARL: Now they're singing again . . .

PRIEST: I was told to report to you.

KARL: What do you want?

PRIEST: I was told to report to you.

KARL: Tell me one thing —

PRIEST: What's that?

KARL: Forget it . . . You swore a false oath. Why did you swear a false oath? You denied the God whom you wear round your neck. For twenty years, you told us, for twenty years you have lived, prayed, served in this monastery —

PRIEST: Yes, I have.

KARL: Before the cock crows! That's more or less what it says, isn't it? Before the cock crows . . . Why did you do it?

PRIEST: Let every man worry about his own guilt.

KARL: In an hour it will be night . . . tell me one thing: if I go in this direction, on and on, through forests, across heathland, on and on, if I swim the rivers, on and on, if I wade through the marshes, on and on, as long as it is night, on and on, on and on, where shall I get to?

(The Priest remains silent)

Speak! Where shall I get to? Speak! It will save your life.

(The Priest remains silent)

I'm going. Betray me! I'm going to my mother. Tell them, I'm going to my mother!

(Karl leaves)

PRIEST: My place is here. I shan't betray you. Your flight won't save me, any more than it will save you. Every road you travel on earth will bring you back here.

SCENE 2

Maria with the child.

MARIA: *Ladybird, ladybird, fly away home,*
Your house is on fire, your children have gone.
All but one, her name is Ann . . .

In the spring, when the snow melts, in the spring Karl will come. That's your father. You've never seen him. That's why I'm telling you, my child. A good father, a dear father, he will take you on his knee, hoppity-hoppity-hop! And he has eyes like you, my child, as clear and blue as a lake. And he can laugh, your father; he will lift you onto his shoulders, you little mite, you can hang on to his hair, hoppity-hoppity-hop! . . .

Ladybird, ladybird, fly away home,
Your house is on fire, your children have gone . . .

Oh God, whatever happens, one day it will be spring. The earth is thousands of years old; spring has never yet failed to come, whatever men did — water drips from the trees, that's the snow melting, because the sun is shining on the earth. It doesn't shine everywhere; behind the woods there is shadow for a long time, there it is cool and wet, when you walk past the soil squelches, the leaves of lost autumns still lie there rotting . . . But the sky, oh, between the trunks you see sky everywhere, an ocean of blue, we stand in the wind, we wear the sun like melting silver in our hair, the dark ploughed fields gape open for light, and the farmhands scatter manure, the horses steam, the brooks gurgle . . . In the spring, when the snow melts, in the spring Karl will come! The evenings by the open window will come, light evenings echoing with the twittering of birds, it's as if you felt the air, the anguished excitement of the buds, the expanse of the fields . . . Oh child, how lovely it is on earth, how lovely it is on earth!

(The Teacher has come in)

MARIA: I think he's asleep.

TEACHER: I've come from the bomb site.

MARIA: Yes?

TEACHER: They still haven't found her.

MARIA: In the spring, when Karl comes, what will he say if he doesn't see his mother any more?

TEACHER: Yes.

MARIA: In the spring, when Karl comes.

TEACHER: I talked to them again . . .

MARIA: Talked to who?

TEACHER: They're foreigners, prisoners of war, really one isn't supposed to talk to them . . .

MARIA: What did they say?

TEACHER: One of them, a prisoner, told me he was buried himself once, for twenty hours, right at the beginning of the war.

MARIA: Well?

TEACHER: That's all. Now they've given up.

NOW THEY'RE SINGING AGAIN

MARIA: Have they stopped digging?

TEACHER: It's fifty hours since it fell. They've stopped digging. I was told they've been put to work at other places, where people may still be alive under the rubble —

MARIA: They've stopped digging.

TEACHER: That's why I came back. I stood down there for fifty hours. I long ago gave up any hope that Mother might still be alive. The rubble is compressed and frozen so hard they had to bore. I gave up all hope long ago, God knows . . . Now they've stopped digging; now I suddenly think, at this moment — could Mother still be alive after all?

MARIA: Mummy!

(Maria sobs)

Why did it have to happen? Tell me that. What harm had Mother ever done anyone? A person like Mummy! . . . Tell me that.

TEACHER: I know.

MARIA: Why did it have to happen?

TEACHER: They're devils.

MARIA: What in the world do they want from us?

TEACHER: They're devils . . . they can't tolerate our superiority. That's all. They can't tolerate the fact that we want to improve the world, that we are able to improve the world. They're devils.

(Maria listens)

MARIA: Was that a knock?

TEACHER: Who can it be — ?

NOW THEY'RE SINGING AGAIN

MARIA: I don't know.

TEACHER: I'm not at home —

MARIA: Suppose it's Karl?

TEACHER: You always think that, every time there's a knock, for the last year —

(Maria goes to the door)

TEACHER: They're devils. Devils. I should like to see them, just once, face to face.

(Maria and Liesel, enter. Liesel is carrying a flowerpot)

MARIA: It's only Liesel.

LIESEL: Teacher . . . Sir —

MARIA: She has brought you a flowerpot.

LIESEL: Because of your wife.

TEACHER: Who knows, Liesel, if she isn't still alive at this moment?

LIESEL: They're not actually flowers, sir. Not at this time of year! There's a bulb in it; in the spring, if all goes well, a tulip will come up.

MARIA: We thank you.

(She puts the flowerpot on the table)

LIESEL: Will those days ever come back again, sir?

TEACHER: What days?

LIESEL: You took us through the Old Town, through the castles and galleries; you explained the pictures to us, so that we shall never forget all the things you found to say about a famous old painting! You gave us eyes for beauty, you know, for nobility and all that.

TEACHER: How's Herbert?

LIESEL: My brother is at the front. At the moment they're in a monastery, he writes, there are medieval frescoes: our teacher would be amazed, he writes.

TEACHER: Herbert was my best pupil.

LIESEL: You always say that.

TEACHER: Herbert was the best pupil I ever had in my life, and he could play the cello; for a time we used to play together a lot, your brother and I, every week —

LIESEL: I know.

(She suddenly turns to Maria)

Do you know that Karl is in the town?

MARIA: Karl?

LIESEL: I'm quite sure it was him, quite sure —

MARIA: Karl?

TEACHER: My son?

MARIA: Where? When? That's impossible.

LIESEL: Last night, I was turning the corner, just over there where your mother lies buried under the rubble, when we suddenly ran into each other. Because it was dark. Sorry, he said —

MARIA: Our Karl?

LIESEL: It was his voice, I'm quite sure, otherwise I shouldn't have recognized him at all. Karl? I said — but he was already gone.

TEACHER: Don't get your hopes up, Maria. It was a mistake; Karl is at the front, many miles from here —

LIESEL: Hasn't he been to see you, then?

MARIA: He's coming home on leave in the spring, he wrote, in the spring . . .

TEACHER: Let us talk no more about it.

LIESEL: Aren't you glad Karl is in the town?

MARIA: Oh Karl!

TEACHER: You see, now she's crying.

MARIA: We have a child and he hasn't seen him yet. He'll get leave in the spring, he always said, and then in autumn came the new offensive.

LIESEL: Perhaps I was really mistaken.

TEACHER: We have hoped so much already; we hope more and more blindly. It would have been better, Liesel, if you'd said nothing.

LIESEL: It gave me a shock too; it wasn't till later that it struck me, he hadn't recognized me in the darkness — it wasn't till later that I ran after him. Karl? I called out . . .

MARIA: You met him again?

LIESEL: I thought so, yes; but when I finally caught up with him, it was someone else —

TEACHER: You see!

LIESEL: I thought myself that I had been mistaken. I thought so myself. I went back and over there on the corner I met him again, the same man who almost knocked me down before. Karl? I said. Don't you recognize me?

MARIA: What happened?

LIESEL: I held him by the sleeve; but he didn't stop. Karl! I said. Karl! And I didn't let go of him. I recognize you, Karl, what's the matter with you?

NOW THEY'RE SINGING AGAIN

MARIA: Was it him?

LIESEL: I saw him as close as you are now, last night —

TEACHER: That's impossible.

MARIA: Last night?

TEACHER: That's impossible; if he had been here he would have come to see us, our Karl wouldn't go wandering round the town like a ghost.

LIESEL: Karl? he said at last, coming to a stop. My name isn't Karl, you're out of luck, my dear child, try it on some other man! And he gave me a crack across the fingers that made me let go at once . . .

(Sirens are heard in the distance)

MARIA: Now they're coming again!

TEACHER: We'll go down into the cellar.

MARIA: Now they're coming again, and the little one has just gone to sleep —

TEACHER: They're devils, devils!

LIESEL: Perhaps I really made a mistake . . .

(They put out the light in the room)

TEACHER: They're devils, I'd just like to see them once: face to face —

SCENE 3

Seven young airmen are waiting to go on operations; lighthearted dance music is coming from a loudspeaker; they are sitting in modern tubular steel chairs, reading, smoking, playing chess or writing letters.

FLYING-OFFICER: Check!

THE OTHER: I don't think they'll get round to us any more tonight. It's past twenty hours already.

FLYING-OFFICER: Check, I said.

THE OTHER: I could see that coming, my dear fellow. It'll cost me a knight. And you your queen.

FLYING-OFFICER: What do you mean?

THE OTHER: It's your move.

(He lights a cigarette)

I really don't think they'll get round to us tonight . . . besides, it's coming down in torrents outside.

(He smokes)

FLYING-OFFICER: Check!

(On the radio, the dance music is suddenly replaced by a chorale from the St. Matthew Passion *by Johann Sebastian Bach)*

RADIO OPERATOR: Switch it off!

NOW THEY'RE SINGING AGAIN

EDWARD: Why?

RADIO OPERATOR: Switch it off! I said. Switch it off!

(The music is turned down)

I can't stomach that kind of music.

EDWARD: I'm simply trying to see what's on the air. In spite of everything, I find that kind of music beautiful . . .

RADIO OPERATOR: That's not the point.

EDWARD: What is the point?

RADIO OPERATOR: Let me write my letter! I don't want to depart this life before I've told the bitch what I think of her . . . You said it yourself: In spite of everything, I find it beautiful. In spite of everything! So do I.

EDWARD: Well then.

RADIO OPERATOR: That's not the point!

EDWARD: What is the point? . . . That it's German music? Music is the best thing they do.

(The Radio Operator writes his letter in silence)

I shan't switch off until you tell me your reasons.

RADIO OPERATOR: Beauty makes me want to vomit.

EDWARD: A very good reason!

RADIO OPERATOR: The world isn't beautiful. What such music tries to make us believe in doesn't exist. Do you understand? It's an illusion.

EDWARD: Maybe . . .

RADIO OPERATOR: The world isn't beautiful.

EDWARD: But music is beautiful. I mean, there is the beauty of an illusion, as you call it. What have we gained, if we rid the world of that too? In the last resort, it's the only thing our bombs can't shatter.

RADIO OPERATOR: That — and your silly jokes.

EDWARD: That's not a joke, my friend.

RADIO OPERATOR: What is it then?

EDWARD: I believe in the illusion. The things that never appear in the world, the things you can't hold with your hands and can't destroy with your hands, the things that only appear as a wish, as a longing, as a goal above and beyond all that exists, these things too have their power over the nations.

RADIO OPERATOR: Do you believe that?

EDWARD: Let his kingdom come! Nothing is more real than this illusion. It built the cathedrals, it smashed the cathedrals, millennia have sung, suffered, murdered for this kingdom that never comes — and yet it is responsible for the whole of human history! Nothing on earth is more real than this illusion.

(A third man, who has been drawing on a cigarette packet, speaks)

BENJAMIN: I believe that too.

RADIO OPERATOR: What?

BENJAMIN: Every war has a purpose. This war too. Otherwise it would all be senseless, a crime, what we are doing. The purpose of this war is to make peace better, above all for us workers. Above all for us workers . . .

(A brief silence of embarrassment over this naive remark)

RADIO OPERATOR: I knew a man who played that kind of music marvellously. It was before the war, when we weren't enemies yet, he and I. In fact we thought we were friends! He talked about that kind of music in a way that astounded me, so intelligently, so nobly, with such sincerity, you know, with such sincerity! And yet it is the same man who shoots hundreds of hostages and burns women and children to death — exactly the same man who played the cello with such sincerity, such deep sincerity . . .

(He seals the envelope, rises)

His name was Herbert.

EDWARD: What do you mean by that?

RADIO OPERATOR: You haven't lost your mother, your father, your little sister. Don't talk! You haven't seen it with your own eyes — they're devils, devils . . .

(A Leading Aircraftman has come in)

FLIGHT-LIEUTENANT: What is it?

AIRCRAFTMAN: Operations —

FLIGHT-LIEUTENANT: When?

AIRCRAFTMAN: Twenty hours fifty.

FLIGHT-LIEUTENANT: Thanks.

(The Flight-Lieutenant gets up and slowly knocks out his pipe)

You heard that?

(Pause)

THE OTHER: Twenty fifty hours, did he say?

FLYING-OFFICER: We shall be finished long before that. It's your move.

NOW THEY'RE SINGING AGAIN

THE OTHER: That's the third time this week!

FLYING-OFFICER: Go on, move.

THE OTHER: I had a ghastly dream last night . . . Our crate caught fire, we jumped out, one, two, three, four, five, I've dreamed the same thing often before: it's as though the parachute just wouldn't float down to earth, and in the end I always land in my home town, and it's like on a Sunday, the town's a bit dreary, dull, unfamiliar, rather as though you had come back centuries later, the streets you used to know have turned into a meadow and there are goats grazing in it, but the café is open to the sky like a ruin, your friends are sitting there reading the paper, and there's moss growing on the little marble tables, moss, no one knows who you are, you've no common memories, no common language and so on . . . a ghastly dream!

FLYING-OFFICER: Come on, move.

(The Flight-Lieutenant puts on his jacket)

FLIGHT-LIEUTENANT: Benjamin?

BENJAMIN: Sir?

FLIGHT-LIEUTENANT: I think we'll just call you Benjamin. You're the youngest of us, Benjamin . . . That doesn't mean you have to stand up.

BENJAMIN: I'm no younger than lots of others.

FLIGHT-LIEUTENANT: One gets used to it, you'll see.

BENJAMIN: Gets used to what?

FLIGHT-LIEUTENANT: It's just a routine job like anything else. There's our Flying-Officer who's always playing chess when he hasn't got a girl, and always losing . . . Thomas over there at the back is drawing the house that every worker will get when the war's over . . . This is the first time you've been on ops, isn't it?

NOW THEY'RE SINGING AGAIN

BENJAMIN: Yes.

FLIGHT-LIEUTENANT: I didn't say that to cheer you up — about its being a routine job. You get used to anything. I'm the eldest, a bit of an oldie, because this is my fifth year at it. Before the war I used to run my father's business, we deal in wool, that used to be a bit of a bore too sometimes —

BENJAMIN: I don't feel scared!

FLIGHT-LIEUTENANT: Scared!

BENJAMIN: Perhaps that makes you smile.

FLIGHT-LIEUTENANT: That's something else you'll find out, Benjamin. There are some things we never talk about. Taboo! Nobody asks whether anyone else feels scared or not.

BENJAMIN: I didn't mean I feel brave! I don't feel brave either, I don't think. Neither scared nor brave. I don't know myself yet.

FLIGHT-LIEUTENANT: How old are you?

BENJAMIN: Twenty. That's to say, twenty and a half.

FLIGHT-LIEUTENANT: Give my best wishes to your girl when you write to her. Things were better for us when we were twenty.

BENJAMIN: I don't write to any girl.

FLIGHT-LIEUTENANT: Why not?

BENJAMIN: Because I don't know any.

FLIGHT-LIEUTENANT: Who're you kidding, Benjamin?

BENJAMIN: As soon as I left school the war broke out —

FLIGHT-LIEUTENANT: I've watched you writing, for two hours at a stretch, Benjamin; a man only writes like that to a girl, a very dear, very sweet girl.

BENJAMIN: I'm not writing to anyone.

FLIGHT-LIEUTENANT: Does that mean — that you're a poet?

BENJAMIN: I should like to become one, sir — if the war doesn't finish us off.

(The Flight-Lieutenant is called)

FLIGHT-LIEUTENANT: Coming —

(The Flight-Lieutenant goes)

FLYING-OFFICER: I refuse to give in.

THE OTHER: We'll never get finished. I tell you, you've lost.

FLYING-OFFICER: We'll see!

THE OTHER: There's nothing you can do about it.

FLYING-OFFICER: We'll leave the board just as it is and play it off tomorrow. It's my move.

(They put their jackets on)

RADIO OPERATOR: And what about all the other things that have happened? I didn't want to believe them either, my friend, life's more comfortable that way, I know! I didn't want to believe them either: dead men with meat hooks in their lower jaws, children's shoes with cut-off children's feet in them —

EDWARD: Stop it!

RADIO OPERATOR: I didn't want to believe these things either. And yet, my friend, and yet they happened: thousands, hundreds of thousands gassed, burned away in lime, wiped out like vermin . . .

EDWARD: Stop it, I said!

RADIO OPERATOR: The world isn't beautiful.

NOW THEY'RE SINGING AGAIN

EDWARD: Do you think we're going to make it more beautiful tonight?

RADIO OPERATOR: What are we to do? I ask you. Are we to let ourselves be killed?

EDWARD: Our bombs don't make them any better — or us either.

RADIO OPERATOR: Try doing it with music! Just try it!

EDWARD: I'm trying to think, that's all.

RADIO OPERATOR: There's nothing else we can do!

EDWARD: Perhaps not. That's the curse . . .

(Silence)

RADIO OPERATOR: When my mother, my father, my little sister were still alive . . . God knows, I thought no differently from you. There is only one justice on earth, justice for all. There is only one freedom that deserves the name, freedom for all. There is only one peace, peace for all —

EDWARD: And now?

RADIO OPERATOR: Oh, I felt so wise when I thought that!

EDWARD: And now: now you've lost everything — ending with your own understanding?

RADIO OPERATOR: It's not understanding; you can't call an idea understanding which doesn't stand up to experience! It's a wish, a dream, a big word —

EDWARD: We gave the big word to the world: we talked about justice and what we bring is force, we talked about peace and what we create is once more hate . . .

RADIO OPERATOR: You haven't lost your mother, your father, your little sister . . . You haven't seen it with your own eyes. They shot my father outside the front door, before he could ask what had happened; they drove my mother and my little sister into the church, the whole village, women, girls, babes at the breast, then they burnt the church down with flame throwers . . . You haven't seen it with your own eyes. Oh, how I envy people like you.

(Edward says nothing)

I also try to think, God knows, not a day passes — I think to myself that all this must and will be avenged.

EDWARD: Avenged?

RADIO OPERATOR: It isn't our vengeance —

EDWARD: Whose is it then?

RADIO OPERATOR: You can't spit in the face of mankind and expect it not to come back upon you, upon your own mother, upon your own children . . . It isn't our vengeance . . . What would their lies, their arrogance, their megalomania matter to us if we didn't end up as their victims? There would be nicer things to do, I know, like playing the fiddle, reading books, riding horses, having children —

EDWARD: Perhaps that would be more use.

RADIO OPERATOR: There can be no peace with Satan, if you live on the same planet. There is only one thing to do: to be stronger than Satan!

EDWARD: To suppress, you mean — to suppress whole peoples . . .

RADIO OPERATOR: To exterminate, I mean, to exterminate!

EDWARD: Exterminate?

RADIO OPERATOR: There's no alternative —

(The Radio Operator is ready for operations, while Edward is still lacing up his equipment)

EDWARD: I don't believe in force, never, not even if one day it is in our hands. No force can exterminate Satan —

RADIO OPERATOR: Why not?

EDWARD: Wherever there is force there will be Satan too.

RADIO OPERATOR: Don't preach! Don't dream! You haven't seen it with your own eyes — they're devils! . . .

(The Flight-Lieutenant comes back carrying a map)

FLIGHT-LIEUTENANT: Men!

(They fall in)

Our orders are not easy. Our orders are as follows:

(Benjamin remains on one side)

BENJAMIN: Strange thoughts are coming into my mind. Perhaps we shall crash to our deaths, suddenly, and for a long time we shan't realize that this is death. For a long time we shan't know where we are. We shall meet the girl who dies at the same time. Perhaps we killed her. It will be the life we could have lived together; it will be remorse, in which we shall all find ourselves . . . That's what it will be.

FLIGHT-LIEUTENANT: Benjamin?

(Benjamin falls in with the rest)

Our orders are as follows:

SCENE 4

Karl and his father, the Senior Teacher.

KARL: Mother is dead —

TEACHER: You still can't believe it, Karl.

KARL: Mother is dead —

TEACHER: That's the way it all is, yes. She was looking forward to your leave. In the spring Karl will be here, she was always saying, in the spring —

KARL: Don't let's talk about it.

TEACHER: She was buried under the rubble; they still haven't found her.

KARL: What else?

TEACHER: You ask, what else? . . .

KARL: In the spring, when the snow melts, I shall have leave. Many mothers will be dead by the spring, when the snow melts . . .

TEACHER: You're talking wildly. What's the matter with you?

KARL: Where's Maria?

TEACHER: Maria is alive.

KARL: Tell me the truth!

TEACHER: Maria is alive, Maria is upstairs.

KARL: Maria is alive . . .

TEACHER: Your little one is well too.

KARL: Maria is upstairs . . .

TEACHER: We told you all that in our letters, Karl; her house was hit, but fortunately Maria wasn't at home. Now she is living with us, together with your child.

KARL: That's the way it all is.

TEACHER: Yes.

KARL: Mother is dead and I didn't see her again, and Maria is at home waiting for my leave, when the snow melts, and I shan't see Maria again either . . .

TEACHER: Karl! What are you talking about, Karl?

KARL: That's the way it is.

TEACHER: God in heaven —

KARL: Leave him out of it.

TEACHER: God in heaven, what's happened, Karl? I come down into the cellar and find my son hiding. How did you get here? I ask you for the third time, how did you get here?

KARL: On foot.

TEACHER: Why are you hiding down here, Karl, when you're on leave and Maria is waiting for you, we're all waiting for you —

KARL: I'm not on leave.

TEACHER: Then why are you here?

KARL: Don't you understand?

(The Teacher stares at him)

I left.

TEACHER: Karl?

KARL: I left . . . on foot . . .

TEACHER: Do you know what that means?

KARL: Better than you.

(Brief silence; Karl lights a cigarette)

TEACHER: If there's an air-raid warning now and the people come down into the cellar, they'll see you, they know you — do you realize what that means?

KARL: Why shouldn't we get to know one another at last?

TEACHER: Do you realize what you're doing?

KARL: I realize what I've done, I alone, because I did it, a week ago today, I, Karl, your only son, I, who had a wife myself, had a child, had a mother who was buried under the rubble at the same time. What does it matter? They weren't the first . . .

TEACHER: Karl, return to your unit at once!

KARL: Never again.

TEACHER: Before people see you, Karl. Tell them you got confused, you lost your way, you —

KARL: Stop talking.

TEACHER: I beg you, Karl, I beseech you, I, your father. Don't you hear me? You've lost your head, my dear Karl, pull yourself together, that's the only thing that can save you, you and us, Maria, your father — return to your unit at once!

(Karl looks at him without a word)

Don't you hear me?

KARL: Have you ever fired on women and children?

TEACHER: Return to your unit at once.

KARL: There's nothing easier; they double up, almost slowly, they fall sideways, mostly, some of them fall backwards. What does it matter? Have you ever fired on women and children, and they sang while you did it? They sang while you did it?

(He begins to sing, the song of the hostages, which fills the cellar with a hollow, rumbling echo)

TEACHER: Someone may hear you! If someone comes in and sees you we're lost.

KARL: I know.

TEACHER: Have you come to hand us all over to the authorities?

KARL: We're lost, Father, even if no one sees us. Be sure of that.

TEACHER: Karl, listen to me —

KARL: It's the only thing we can be sure of.

TEACHER: I can understand you —

KARL: That's impossible; you didn't do it.

TEACHER: Karl, you were obeying orders! I tell you, we're not to blame —

KARL: Do you still believe that?

TEACHER: Karl! Karl!

KARL: Don't start getting solemn.

TEACHER: Gather your wits together, Karl, and listen to me for two minutes, just two minutes, and then decide what you want to do —

(He sits down beside his son)

KARL: I know exactly what you're going to say.

TEACHER: I too, Karl, have been ordered to do things that I would never have done of my own free will, that I would never have done on my own responsibility; it started with small, insignificant things, as you know; and why did I do them?

KARL: Where there is no courage there are always plenty of excuses.

TEACHER: I did it for your sake, for Mother's sake! At that time I had the choice of becoming a senior teacher or of being out of work, penniless and starving. You're laughing!

KARL: I'm not laughing —

TEACHER: At that time we were governed by terror, by the utmost terror, and besides there was a lot of good in it too, and as I told you, I did it for your sake, for Mother's sake.

KARL: Mother is buried under the rubble —

TEACHER: For your sake, Karl! I didn't want you to have to pay for it, I didn't want your whole youth to be ruined —

KARL: It has been ruined.

TEACHER: I said yes. Later it was no longer a question of one's job and one's living, it was a question of whether one still had a home on this earth or not, and I said yes again, because I didn't want to rob you of your home. Do you understand me?

KARL: Go on.

TEACHER: Each time I was only trying to do the best under the circumstances, Karl —

KARL: Let's say, the most advantageous.

TEACHER: I was thinking of you and Mother. You know now what it means to have a wife, to have a child —

KARL: Go on.

TEACHER: Later it was no longer a question of having a home or being an outsider, gradually one's very life was at stake, and I said yes, Karl; that too is a matter of conscience, one doesn't kill one's wife for the sake of one's own personal convictions, one's wife, one's son —

KARL: It's better to kill others!

(He stands up again)

Have you ever fired on women and children?

TEACHER: I tell you, you were obeying orders!

KARL: And who gave the orders?

TEACHER: You're not to blame, Karl, we're none of us to blame for the orders we're given —

KARL: That's just the point!

TEACHER: You're laughing? . . .

KARL: Every word you utter accuses us. — Obedience is no excuse, even if we make obedience our ultimate virtue it doesn't free us from responsibility, nothing frees us from responsibility, we are given responsibility, each his own; we cannot pass it on to someone else to manage for us. We cannot cast off the burden of personal freedom — and that's just what we have tried to do, and that's precisely where our guilt lies.

(Silence)

There is no going back, Father, be sure of that.

(Sirens sound in the distance)

TEACHER: That's the air-raid warning.

KARL: Again.

TEACHER: Now people will come down here . . . Karl . . . Did I take all that on myself so that in the end it should prove to have been for nothing?

KARL: I see no way out, Father, not for any of us. We're guilty.

TEACHER: Return to your unit . . . Any minute now people will come down into the cellar . . . Maria mustn't see you either; if Maria sees you she won't leave you till we're lost.

KARL: Maria!

TEACHER: Karl, I beg you for our lives.

KARL: Now she is coming down the stairs, Maria, and our child whom I have never seen . . . now they're coming down the stairs . . .

(He grips his father)

Father, look after them!

(Karl disappears before the people come)

LIESEL: He's here already . . . Maria, the teacher is already down here! So come on.

A WOMAN: That's the third time, the third time today.

BLOCK WARDEN: Stop talking, will you!

THE WOMAN: I only said, that's the third time . . .

NOW THEY'RE SINGING AGAIN

BLOCK WARDEN: We know that as well as you do.

THE WOMAN: Heavens above, we spend every night sitting in the cellar, every other day, we're not even allowed to talk — who do you think you are anyway?

BLOCK WARDEN: I'm a block warden.

THE WOMAN: I'm a human being —

SOMEONE: We're all human beings.

THE WOMAN: You'll be forbidding me to breathe next, you'll be forbidding me to do anything. What are we fighting this war for, I'd like to know? —

SOMEONE: Read the papers!

THE WOMAN: What for?

SOMEONE: Read the papers . . .

THE WOMAN: If you're not allowed to breathe, not allowed to talk, not allowed to put on the light, not allowed to do anything, why don't we let ourselves be killed? We're not even allowed to do that . . .

BLOCK WARDEN: All panic must be avoided. That's my duty, that's what I've been trained for, that's what I'm responsible for —

THE WOMAN: And I tell you it's coming just the same!

BLOCK WARDEN: What is?

THE WOMAN: The third wave!

(The sound of bombs falling is heard in the distance)

BLOCK WARDEN: My God, we're lucky again, it's not in our district this time either . . .

TEACHER: Don't cry, Maria.

LIESEL: She's always afraid the baby is dead; he's only sleeping.

TEACHER: Don't cry, Maria. It's all over; it's all over for this time.

LIESEL: It's wonderful how he sleeps; he doesn't hear any of it. Do you see how he's moving his tiny fingers? You little mite! Don't you see how he's breathing?

MARIA: Yes, yes.

LIESEL: Such a sweet tot! . . . He's really breathing.

THE WOMAN: How old is he?

MARIA: A year, almost a year . . .

THE WOMAN: He won't remember anything about this war when he's big. Just think of that! He'll see where our town used to stand, yes, he'll see that — but he won't remember anything himself — that means a great deal, you know, that means a great deal. Wherever there is no one left who can remember this war from his own experience, life will start again!

SOMEONE: Or the next war.

THE WOMAN: Why that?

SOMEONE: Because there'll be no one left who can remember what war is like.

(The Woman pricks up her ears)

THE WOMAN: Do you hear? That's the ambulance —

BLOCK WARDEN: Devil take you!

THE WOMAN: Aren't I allowed to say that either?

BLOCK WARDEN: If you don't keep your stupid trap shut —

THE WOMAN: What will you do?

NOW THEY'RE SINGING AGAIN

BLOCK WARDEN: I shall have to have you arrested, do you understand, I shall have to. If I don't, someone else can report me. You mustn't think only of yourself, woman! I've got a wife too...

(Again and again an indistinct noise is heard)

MARIA: If only spring would come, if only spring would come!

TEACHER: Spring is sure to come.

MARIA: In spring Karl will be here, then we shan't have to stay in the town, we shall go out into the forest, we can very well do that, even if it's raining, we can live in the forest... When we met, on his last leave, when we went out in the canvas canoe, we lived in the forest, for days on end, oh, it was wonderful!

TEACHER: I'm sure it was.

MARIA: If it were only spring again, just once more!...

(An Old Man has come in whom obviously no one knows; eventually he turns to someone at random — the Teacher)

OLD MAN: The cathedral has been hit.

BLOCK WARDEN: That doesn't matter.

OLD MAN: How do you mean?

BLOCK WARDEN: It will all be rebuilt.

OLD MAN: Who by?

BLOCK WARDEN: More beautiful than before! After the war.

OLD MAN: Yes, yes, of course...

THE WOMAN: Are they dropping phosphorus again?

OLD MAN: People are running down the street —

BLOCK WARDEN: Be quiet!

NOW THEY'RE SINGING AGAIN

OLD MAN: But I saw it myself.

BLOCK WARDEN: Blathering about it doesn't help!

OLD MAN: Nor does keeping quiet.

THE WOMAN: Perhaps he's right, grandad, we shouldn't talk about it, any of us, we shouldn't ever talk again.

OLD MAN: *(Talking to himself)* People are running down the street, but they can't get through the burning tar; in a minute they're all charred . . . they stand there like black tree trunks in the street . . .

TEACHER: Where are you going, Maria? Where are you going?

MARIA: I must get out —

TEACHER: It's madness!

MARIA: I want to go into the forest —

TEACHER: Not now!

MARIA: We're suffocating here, I think, we're suffocating here —

TEACHER: Not now! Maria, do you hear me?

MARIA: I hear, I hear —

(Bombs are heard nearby)

SOMEONE: Incendiaries. Those are incendiary bombs, they'll soon be over.

(An Air-Raid Warden appears in the doorway)

AIR-RAID WARDEN: Teacher, your son —

MARIA: Karl!

AIR-RAID WARDEN: Your son is outside — he has hanged himself . . .

TEACHER: My son.

AIR-RAID WARDEN: The street is on fire!

(The Air-Raid Warden hurries away again)

TEACHER: Maria! Where has she gone to?

(He goes after Maria, who has run out with the child)

THE WOMAN: She's crazy. I saw it coming. She's always afraid the child is going to suffocate.

SOMEONE: Is that her husband who hanged himself?

LIESEL: It was him after all. Our Karl . . .

OLD MAN: They're running down the street, but the street's on fire, they can't get through the tar, in a minute they're charred, they stand there like black tree trunks in the street.

(The Teacher has come back. The noise dies away)

TEACHER: The street's on fire.

THE WOMAN: God punish the enemy! God punish the enemy! God punish the enemy!

SOMEONE: Our boys do exactly the same.

BLOCK WARDEN: Who said that?

THE WOMAN: I didn't.

BLOCK WARDEN: Who said that? A coward, who doesn't own up, a traitor who would be stood against the wall if he owned up.

TEACHER: Our boys do exactly the same.

BLOCK WARDEN: You?

THE WOMAN: That isn't true —

BLOCK WARDEN: We know you, teacher, you didn't say that.

TEACHER: Our boys do exactly the same. I'm saying it now: Our boys do exactly the same.

(Absolute silence)

BLOCK WARDEN: I must ask you for your name, you understand, I must . . .

PART TWO

SCENE 5

The Priest stands cutting bread which he places on a stone table; the song of the hostages is heard.

PRIEST: Now they're singing again . . . God give them rest!

(A Child has appeared; the Priest counts the slices of bread)

CHILD: Little Father.

PRIEST: What is it?

CHILD: Now they're shooting again!

PRIEST: Fourteen, fifteen, sixteen, seventeen . . . Nothing more can happen to us, my child. That's the war that is still going on. Tell them nothing more can happen to us.

CHILD: We're all singing.

PRIEST: I can hear it. — Take this jug, my child. This is the wine, this is the blood of Our Lord, and tell them I'll bring the bread.

CHILD: How good you are, Little Father.

(The Child leaves carrying the jug)

PRIEST: Seventeen, eighteen, nineteen, twenty, twenty-one — that's how they stood, twenty-one in a row, and that's how they sang, as they're singing now.

NOW THEY'RE SINGING AGAIN

(Meanwhile the airmen have also appeared: the Flight-Lieutenant, wearing a white first-aid bandage, the Flying-Officer, the Leading Aircraftman, the Radio Operator)

FLIGHT-LIEUTENANT: God be with you.

PRIEST: God be with you too.

FLIGHT-LIEUTENANT: I hope we're not intruding here.

PRIEST: Let us hope not.

(Short pause)

FLIGHT-LIEUTENANT: Who's that singing?

PRIEST: There are a lot of people, sir, a lot of people —

FLIGHT-LIEUTENANT: I can hear that. A choir. I love choirs; we've heard that song on the radio. But I mean, what kind of people are they?

PRIEST: I didn't know them.

FLIGHT-LIEUTENANT: You didn't?

PRIEST: Whenever they hear shooting, they sing again. God give them rest.

(Short pause)

FLIGHT-LIEUTENANT: How about you?

PRIEST: I give them bread. Sometimes I also catch fish. Then I take them the fish —

FLIGHT-LIEUTENANT: Have you any bread for us, by any chance?

PRIEST: If you're hungry.

FLIGHT-LIEUTENANT: We're all hungry!

NOW THEY'RE SINGING AGAIN

FLYING-OFFICER: Hungry and thirsty!

PRIEST: We've only got wine . . .

FLYING-OFFICER: Red or white?

PRIEST: It's the blood of Our Lord . . .

FLYING-OFFICER: Red then.

PRIEST: Yes.

FLIGHT-LIEUTENANT: Bread and wine, that would be nice! We thank you.

(The Priest goes out)

FLYING-OFFICER: A bit odd, that priest —

AIRCRAFTMAN: Well, for the moment we're under cover, that's the main thing; for the moment we're under cover.

FLYING-OFFICER: That looks to me like a monastery . . . Maybe we'll be lucky, men, the way you read in books; maybe it's a convent. Devil take me, some nuns are hot stuff, just imagine a young thing who only knows sin from praying, who has still got it all to learn! Nothing excites me more than a shy woman; I love it when they resist.

RADIO OPERATOR: He's off again!

FLYING-OFFICER: When the war is over, boys, no one is going to give us our youth back. We must take the women, the young ones, as long as they attract us, and as true as I'm standing in this strange place, they attract me!

(Meanwhile they have sat down)

FLIGHT-LIEUTENANT: I was already thinking to myself, this is death. If this is death, I thought, what have we against it? By the way, you've earned a medal, you lot. I shall inform our Air Marshal as soon as he comes along.

RADIO OPERATOR: I'd rather have a slice of bread.

FLIGHT-LIEUTENANT: Where's Benjamin?

FLYING-OFFICER: Benjamin is here.

FLIGHT-LIEUTENANT: I don't see him —

FLYING-OFFICER: I sent him to spy out the land, it's better to be on the safe side.

FLIGHT-LIEUTENANT: He was a good lad. That was his first flight and his last . . . How did it happen?

RADIO OPERATOR: All in a flash.

FLIGHT-LIEUTENANT: And where's Thomas?

FLYING-OFFICER: He's safe. He jumped before we caught fire.

FLIGHT-LIEUTENANT: He's safe —

RADIO OPERATOR: Edward jumped before we caught fire too.

FLIGHT-LIEUTENANT: How about Alexander?

RADIO OPERATOR: I don't know about him.

FLIGHT-LIEUTENANT: That's a blow for you, Flying-Officer. None of us play chess.

FLYING-OFFICER: That had already occurred to me. It was my move.

AIRCRAFTMAN: I saw him.

FLIGHT-LIEUTENANT: Alexander?

AIRCRAFTMAN: His parachute was on fire.

FLIGHT-LIEUTENANT: Poor fellow . . .

NOW THEY'RE SINGING AGAIN

AIRCRAFTMAN: He was always dreaming that his parachute carried him to his home town.

(Silence)

FLIGHT-LIEUTENANT: Where are we?

RADIO OPERATOR: That's just the question.

AIRCRAFTMAN: For the moment we're under cover, that's the main thing; for the moment we're under cover.

FLIGHT-LIEUTENANT: Bread and wine, it seems to me that we're doing all right for the moment, and we shall find out sooner or later where we are, if we're patient. They don't take us for enemies. That seems certain. And they speak our language too.

(Benjamin comes)

FLIGHT-LIEUTENANT: Well?

BENJAMIN: Sir . . .

FLIGHT-LIEUTENANT: Come on, out with it!

BENJAMIN: I only saw the people who are singing. They're old men, women, and children. They're sitting at a long table, twenty-one altogether, singing, holding their bread in their hands. It's a very strange sight.

FLIGHT-LIEUTENANT: Old men, women and children?

RADIO OPERATOR: Can't we just ask straight out?

AIRCRAFTMAN: What country this is?

RADIO OPERATOR: Yes.

AIRCRAFTMAN: They'll raise the alarm: they'll say the enemy is here. In an hour we shall be prisoners.

FLYING-OFFICER: He's right.

AIRCRAFTMAN: Let's suppose we're a mile from the frontier, or half a mile —

RADIO OPERATOR: Only we must know where the frontier lies, before it's any use to us.

AIRCRAFTMAN: We'll find out.

RADIO OPERATOR: How? Our radio is kaput.

AIRCRAFTMAN: We'll find out. We'll chat about this and that, quite harmless subjects, we'll get the Priest talking — leave it to me!

RADIO OPERATOR: Perhaps we're in our own country —

FLIGHT-LIEUTENANT: Anything's possible.

RADIO OPERATOR: We're in our own country, but we don't ask, we keep under cover, that's the main thing, and one day, when the war's been over for ages, we'll still be sitting in our hideout, the way we were trained, we'll never ask, we'll never find out that we're at home —

AIRCRAFTMAN: At home, did you say — among all these ruins?

RADIO OPERATOR: Do you imagine our homes look very different?

BENJAMIN: Quiet! —

FLYING-OFFICER: Is he really bringing us wine and bread?

(The Priest brings wine and bread, accompanied by the Child; he distributes the bread)

PRIEST: That's all we have left.

FLIGHT-LIEUTENANT: We thank you!

PRIEST: We must bake some more, as soon as you've eaten this.

NOW THEY'RE SINGING AGAIN

(The airmen stand eating the bread and drinking the wine in silence; each one takes a large or a small gulp from the jug and passes it on)

CHILD: Little Father?

PRIEST: They won't do you any harm.

CHILD: When will the shooting stop?

PRIEST: I don't know, my child. It can do us no more harm. You need have no fear; no bullet can ever strike you again, my child.

CHILD: Who are these men?

PRIEST: I don't know them.

CHILD: Were they the enemy?

PRIEST: I don't know, my child; now they're hungry.

CHILD: Everyone is hungry . . .

PRIEST: Take this jug, it's empty, and fetch the other one.

(The Child obeys)

FLIGHT-LIEUTENANT: Is that your own child, Little Father?

PRIEST: No.

(The Child brings the other jug)

AIRCRAFTMAN: Tell me, was that a monastery?

PRIEST: It was.

AIRCRAFTMAN: Where's the nearest village?

PRIEST: The nearest village —

(He passes on the jug)

The nearest village doesn't exist any more.

AIRCRAFTMAN: Some village must be the nearest!

PRIEST: I don't know it, I can't see it. Still, you're quite right, young man, some village must be the nearest always, no matter how far away it is.

AIRCRAFTMAN: How far is it then?

PRIEST: I don't know the village.

AIRCRAFTMAN: Roughly.

PRIEST: The nearest village I knew used to lie quite close to our monastery; it was burnt down, the inhabitants are dead and nothing more can happen to them. Then come the forests, the fields where the corn used to grow, rye especially, oats too. Then come the marshes, the heathland where the famous battles were always being fought. Perhaps the nearest village but one, which I never knew, has also been burnt down —

AIRCRAFTMAN: Perhaps.

PRIEST: That's how it is. I can't understand it; I can't explain it.

AIRCRAFTMAN: Do you mean to say you don't know yourself how far it is to the nearest village, to the nearest person who is still alive?

PRIEST: I don't know.

AIRCRAFTMAN: Tell me — how can you stand this situation?

PRIEST: My place is here.

AIRCRAFTMAN: Can you stand it?

PRIEST: One has to learn to, young friend. It isn't difficult, when you know that you will never reach the next village.

AIRCRAFTMAN: Never?

PRIEST: My place is here.

NOW THEY'RE SINGING AGAIN

(The Flight-Lieutenant gives the empty jug back to the Child)

FLIGHT-LIEUTENANT: We're to bake bread, you said?

PRIEST: That's right.

FLIGHT-LIEUTENANT: We'll do our best, Little Father. I must admit I've never baked bread in my life and have no idea how it's done —

PRIEST: Oh, it's easy.

FLIGHT-LIEUTENANT: Have any of you ever baked bread?

PRIEST: We'll learn together.

(He turns to the Leading Aircraftman)

The child will show you where the axe is. You'll find wood in all the ruins, charred beams, pieces of pictures with the paint scorched. Just split it neatly, then we can light a fire and bake.

AIRCRAFTMAN: Light a fire and bake —

PRIEST: The child can show you everything.

AIRCRAFTMAN: Little Father!

PRIEST: What is it?

AIRCRAFTMAN: Why did you say just now that we should never reach the next village?

PRIEST: Because that's how it is, friend.

AIRCRAFTMAN: Nothing is so far away that we shan't reach it if we walk and walk, walk and walk. Why do you smile?

PRIEST: Am I smiling?

AIRCRAFTMAN: Do you think you can frighten me?

PRIEST: Am I frightening you?

AIRCRAFTMAN: Nothing is so far that we can't reach it, we who are young. Young! Do you know how young we are? War has taken the years away from us; don't look at our faces! I tell you our life is young, we're still boys who don't know what life is. Life? Doesn't everything that is called life lie in front of us? . . . Oh, what's the sense in talking? . . . You don't frighten me. We have looked death in the eye, more than once, we have flown through walls of fire: next to us, in the middle of the squadron, they cracked up and fell, they split apart like a blazing torch. We know what it is to have our own wings on fire, we know what it is to be struck by a stream of machine-gun bullets from behind: you scarcely hear them, but the friend sitting beside you stops answering and the blood drips from his hair. We know what it is to drop down towards the sea, to go hurtling down towards the sea in the darkness — we have looked death in the eye, more than once!

PRIEST: Why do you tell me that?

AIRCRAFTMAN: I ask you, where is the nearest village? You don't answer.

PRIEST: I don't know.

AIRCRAFTMAN: Where's the nearest village? . . .

(He has drawn his revolver)

Where's the nearest village? . . .

FLIGHT-LIEUTENANT: He's gone crazy.

AIRCRAFTMAN: Where's the nearest village? . . . Where's the nearest village? . . .

(His comrades restrain the raving man)

PRIEST: Nothing more can happen to me.

NOW THEY'RE SINGING AGAIN

(After a period of silence, the Child approaches the Aircraftman and offers him his hand; the Aircraftman follows him)

PRIEST: We must have fresh water too.

FLYING-OFFICER: I'll fetch it.

PRIEST: That's nice of you. I'll show you where our well was —

FLYING-OFFICER: I'll find it!

PRIEST: I don't think so.

FLYING-OFFICER: Are you afraid I'll find your nuns?

PRIEST: It's our only well and it may have been buried under rubble again . . .

RADIO OPERATOR: I'll help.

FLIGHT-LIEUTENANT: War destroys a lot.

(The Priest goes out with the Flying-Officer and the Radio Operator)

FLIGHT-LIEUTENANT: What about you, Benjamin? You don't say a word.

BENJAMIN: I'm listening.

FLIGHT-LIEUTENANT: Where do you think we are? . . . You don't answer.

BENJAMIN: I had no one but Father and Mother. They'll be crying now, they'll say we're dead.

FLIGHT-LIEUTENANT: Dead? . . .

BENJAMIN: That's all more difficult for you others. You have a wife, Flight-Lieutenant, a child of your own, or two, and all the others had a girl friend, even if it was a girl friend they called a bitch because she had left them —

NOW THEY'RE SINGING AGAIN

FLIGHT-LIEUTENANT: You're right: they'll think we're dead, no doubt about it, they'll think we're dead —

(Benjamin listens; the song is heard)

BENJAMIN: Now they're singing again. Women, old men, children, they're sitting at a long table, twenty-one of them altogether, singing, holding their bread in their hands. And with their mouths shut. It's a very strange sight.

(The Flight-Lieutenant comes to a sudden decision)

FLIGHT-LIEUTENANT: Benjamin!

BENJAMIN: Yes sir.

FLIGHT-LIEUTENANT: Go out; look round! Go on until you meet someone, a peasant, a child, a girl, anybody. Look at them, every person you see, talk to them. We'll wait here till you get back. We'll wait in any case.

BENJAMIN: Very good, sir.

FLIGHT-LIEUTENANT: We must know where we are.

BENJAMIN: Very good, sir.

FLIGHT-LIEUTENANT: One more thing . . . If you meet anyone, any living person, whoever he may be, give him this ring.

(Benjamin goes; the Flight-Lieutenant is alone)

FLIGHT-LIEUTENANT: Jenny, Jenny . . . now she's crossing the street with the children, Jenny in black. I'm sure it suits her, and the children will be asking a lot of questions . . . Why? why? why? . . . Jenny will cry. On the last evening we saw each other I was so depressed. I don't know why. I was so depressed.

(The Priest comes back)

PRIEST: This is the mill. It's the only one we have. It's old and you have to grind slowly —

FLIGHT-LIEUTENANT: I understand.

PRIEST: What?

FLIGHT-LIEUTENANT: It seems we have to start from the beginning.

PRIEST: I'll pick the rye for you . . .

(They start work)

FLIGHT-LIEUTENANT: Just think, Little Father, we've never baked our own bread before. You'll have to show us everything. We're absolute beginners, big as we are . . .

PRIEST: We'll learn.

FLIGHT-LIEUTENANT: If Jenny could see me now! My wife's name is Jenny.

PRIEST: You've got a wife?

FLIGHT-LIEUTENANT: A wife and two children, we're a whole family. On the last evening we saw each other I was so depressed, I don't know why . . . I was so depressed . . . A lot of things must be changed! I mean, after the war. We had a big business; we deal in wool. I shall give all that up. My grandfather used to shear his own sheep. I shall go back to the country again with Jenny, not for a picnic, you understand, not just for the holidays. Let others make money and do big business, I shan't envy them any more, that's freedom. Don't you agree? Our cars, our servants, our whole social life — I shall give all that up, and Jenny will be happier . . . You say nothing, Little Father?

PRIEST: I'm listening to you, Flight-Lieutenant.

FLIGHT-LIEUTENANT: A lot of things must be changed. We had a house that was far too big for us, you see. I had it built so that people should envy us. Envy our happiness, but our happiness never came into being. The house was as big as my ambition, you see, and just as empty. I shall give that up too . . . You say nothing, Little Father?

PRIEST: I'm listening to you, Flight-Lieutenant.

FLIGHT-LIEUTENANT: But you say nothing.

PRIEST: We must bake a lot of bread, a lot more guests will be coming.

FLIGHT-LIEUTENANT: Guests?

PRIEST: Don't you hear the gunfire again?

FLIGHT-LIEUTENANT: I hear it less and less. Strange. Perhaps we overestimated that too?

PRIEST: Overestimated what?

FLIGHT-LIEUTENANT: That noise out there.

PRIEST: That's right. You must grind slowly . . . on and on . . .

FLIGHT-LIEUTENANT: Tell me, who is that child who brought us the jug?

PRIEST: I didn't know him.

FLIGHT-LIEUTENANT: He had a strange effect on me. Our own child would have handled the jug in just the same way . . . I love the gestures that will exist always and everywhere, as long as there are human beings, and there will be human beings for at least as long as there are battles —

PRIEST: Undoubtedly —

FLIGHT-LIEUTENANT: Empires crumble, nations awake, they make the history of a decade, a century, states, frontiers, wars. That is the world of events! We talk a lot about it; the newspapers, the radio, the history books speak of nothing else, and the more horrible its events were, the more deadly — the more inclined we were to consider this the real world, the only real world!

PRIEST: It is very real.

FLIGHT-LIEUTENANT: I think we ought to have lived differently, Little Father, quite differently. Anyhow, Jenny and I ought to have . . . Our real life lies in the sight of a child holding a jug, in the sound of the wind in the trees, in the play of a never-ending stream flowing over alien pebbles. — Why didn't we live differently?

PRIEST: I don't know.

FLIGHT-LIEUTENANT: I have a feeling that quite a different world also exists, Little Father . . . a homeland that doesn't separate us. Those who don't have this homeland everywhere, have it nowhere. I don't mean that everything is one. You can't be a brother to others if you abandon yourself . . . I have a feeling that there is a homeland that we ought to have discovered, a homeland stretching all round the world —

(He breaks off, laughs)

I say, we ought to have lived differently — as though I were no longer alive!

(The Aircraftman comes with charred wood and puts it down)

PRIEST: That's right. We shall have to bake a lot of bread . . .

(The Aircraftman goes out again)

PRIEST: Why do you hesitate?

FLIGHT-LIEUTENANT: You keep saying we shall have to bake a lot of bread, but if we go on baking like this all the time, heaven knows where all the corn is coming from.

PRIEST: Yes, the corn.

FLIGHT-LIEUTENANT: Where is it coming from?

PRIEST: I think the living will miss it.

FLIGHT-LIEUTENANT: Will they go hungry?

PRIEST: It's the corn that could have been planted in all the years and all the fields in which there were battles. War killed it. So it's our corn.

FLIGHT-LIEUTENANT: I don't understand.

PRIEST: Well, that's how I think it is.

FLIGHT-LIEUTENANT: Do you mean that Jenny too will go hungry, Little Father? And the children? It's not their fault, is it? It's not their fault?

(The Flying-Officer comes)

FLYING-OFFICER: The well is clear.

PRIEST: That's fine!

FLYING-OFFICER: Now we need the jug —

PRIEST: The child has the jug.

(The Flying-Officer goes)

PRIEST: They're good lads . . .

FLIGHT-LIEUTENANT: How did *you* come to this place?

PRIEST: That was a long time ago.

FLIGHT-LIEUTENANT: When?

PRIEST: It was during the last war, the war before. I was a soldier —

FLIGHT-LIEUTENANT: You too.

PRIEST: I was engaged and I was a soldier. My God, how young we were! I'll wait for you to come back, she said, and even now I still believe that she was beautiful. She waved her red kerchief, the sort peasant girls wear in our part of the world. I never saw her again.

FLIGHT-LIEUTENANT: Why not?

PRIEST: We went to the front, I was wounded and later taken prisoner. I was a prisoner for three years . . . The girl remained faithful to me, even when she thought I was dead. Later, when I came home, she had been living in the convent for a long time. I don't know whether she ever heard that I had come home. We wanted to be farmers like our parents. I don't know whether my fiancée is still alive. I couldn't be closer to her than here.

FLIGHT-LIEUTENANT: In the monastery.

PRIEST: It was always a lonely monastery, a single monk used to live in it, a sick Russian. We built the altar together, that has once more been reduced to ruins. On Sundays he used to sing to the peasants, we helped them with the harvest, we bore the dead to the grave, we made the candles and we had two goats of our own. One day we buried him too, and the peasants sang for him, as well as they could . . . Then, for twelve years, I was alone — until that evening came.

FLIGHT-LIEUTENANT: What evening?

PRIEST: For weeks the foreign tanks rolled past, soldiers came into the monastery, looked at all the cellars and left again; one morning the village was burnt down. In the evening they brought the twenty-one hostages, I had to dig a long grave, then it all went very quickly: they were made to stand by the grave, old men, women, children . . . They sang until the last one was shot.

FLIGHT-LIEUTENANT: Did you hear that yourself, Little Father?

PRIEST: I had to swear that I hadn't heard it.

FLIGHT-LIEUTENANT: And you swore?

PRIEST: Yes.

FLIGHT-LIEUTENANT: A false oath —

PRIEST: Yes.

FLIGHT-LIEUTENANT: Why?

PRIEST: I was afraid. He counted on his fingers. At seven I was afraid. I swore. Later they came back and said: We don't believe in oaths any more!

FLIGHT-LIEUTENANT: With some justification . . .

PRIEST: So I was shot too.

FLIGHT-LIEUTENANT: And now?

(Karl, who hanged himself, has appeared)

KARL: It was I who shot you. I did it on orders . . .

(They do not notice him)

FLIGHT-LIEUTENANT: And now?

PRIEST: It will take a long time; even some of the dead are still thinking of revenge. I'm afraid it will take a long time before there's nothing left.

FLIGHT-LIEUTENANT: What do you mean?

PRIEST: I mean, until there is nothing left of all the terrible things that have happened.

FLIGHT-LIEUTENANT: You speak as though it was their fault that they were misused; are they to be held responsible for the terrible things that happened?

PRIEST: The fact that we died as their victims does not by itself guarantee that we were good people.

FLIGHT-LIEUTENANT: What about those who did it?

PRIEST: Let every man worry about his own guilt.

FLIGHT-LIEUTENANT: Does that mean that you want to forgive the murderers?

PRIEST: I'm not a judge, my friend, I can't even forgive. I was afraid like most people. I shall fish, as well as I can, and I shall bake bread for them as long as they ask for it, as long as they need me —

FLIGHT-LIEUTENANT: And what is all this for?

PRIEST: I think we all have to stay here till we get to know the life that we could have lived together. That is our remorse, our damnation, our redemption.

(Karl has come closer)

KARL: It was I who shot you. I did it on orders . . .

(They do not notice him)

FLIGHT-LIEUTENANT: I understand, Little Father. But I don't know how I'm to tell my men; they're such youngsters.

PRIEST: What is it you have to tell them?

FLIGHT-LIEUTENANT: Benjamin — he wanted to become a poet! He told me so on that last evening, when I talked to him for the first time. Do you think he would have become a poet?

PRIEST: All sorts of things might have happened.

FLIGHT-LIEUTENANT: How am I to tell them that this is death, where we are now; they're not prepared for it — they haven't lived yet.

(The singing is heard)

KARL: Now they're singing again!

(Karl falls to his knees)

FLIGHT-LIEUTENANT: Who is that?

PRIEST: Every road leads him here. His name is Karl, a young man who is looking for his mother.

(Karl cries out)

KARL: It was I who killed you, it was I!

PRIEST: I know, Karl . . . There's a woman here whom you shot; she says she's your mother.

KARL: How is that possible?

PRIEST: Do you want to see her?

KARL: My mother?

PRIEST: Do you want to see her?

KARL: How is that possible?

PRIEST: All mothers are one, Karl, all mothers are one . . . Do you want to see her?

(Karl holds his hands over his eyes)

KARL: God above!

SCENE 6

Maria alone.

MARIA: Maybe the spring is here now . . . Water is dripping from the trees, that's the snow melting; because the sun is shining on the earth. It isn't shining everywhere; the woods remain in shadow for a long time, there it is cool and wet, when you walk past the trees the soil squelches, the leaves of lost autumns still lie there rotting. But the sky, oh, between the trunks you see sky everywhere, an ocean of blue. There's a butterfly . . . You have never seen any of this, my child, that's why I say to you: It is beautiful on earth, especially in the spring, there is a gurgling everywhere, the dark furrows gape open for light, and the farmhands are scattering manure, the horses are steaming . . . You've never seen any of that . . . The couples who are still alive wear the sun like melting silver in their hair. The evenings are warm and light and echo with the twittering of birds; it's as if you felt the air, the anguished excitement of the buds, the expanse of the fields . . . You died, my child, before you could see a bud, a bird hopping at our feet, you didn't even see a crow flying over the brown ploughed land — that's why I say to you: It's beautiful on earth, especially in the spring, there is a gurgling everywhere, that's the snow melting, because the sun is shining on the earth . . .

(Benjamin has appeared)

BENJAMIN: May I ask where we are? I was an airman . . . I haven't found anyone I could ask anywhere. They shot us down — in the middle of the night, when it was raining. That's what happened. Now we don't know where we are. — Yes . . .

MARIA: Why do you stop all of a sudden?

BENJAMIN: You're right.

MARIA: What do you mean?

BENJAMIN: Perhaps we're enemies . . .

MARIA: We don't know each other.

BENJAMIN: I'm very glad you're here! As I tramped through the fields — it was a fine day, I saw the red willows, the last snow lying in the shadows, the horses, the brown fields gulping down the sun, a blue day, a day like sparkling glass, a magnificent day, heaven knows — but I felt as though I were wandering on Mars; I don't feel light-hearted.

MARIA: Didn't you see our peasants scattering manure on the fields, as they do at this time of year?

BENJAMIN: You mean the old man who doesn't hear when you speak to him?

MARIA: The young men aren't in the fields.

BENJAMIN: I shouted to him. I don't think he can hear. I shouted at the top of my voice. I don't think he can see. I showed him the ring . . . It's our Flight-Lieutenant's ring.

(Benjamin sits down beside Maria)

BENJAMIN: I'm glad you can hear me! My name is Benjamin.

MARIA: My name is Maria.

BENJAMIN: Look what I found —

MARIA: What is it?

NOW THEY'RE SINGING AGAIN

BENJAMIN: A fossil, I think.

MARIA: A fossil?

BENJAMIN: We learnt about them at school. This was once a little creature; it lived before there were any human beings, before Adam and Eve —

MARIA: Is that known for a fact?

BENJAMIN: Oh yes, we know a great deal.

MARIA: How?

BENJAMIN: What you are holding in your hand is the ooze of a sea that once covered the land, a very ancient sea. This little creature lived in this sea, it swam about in it, died and sank into the ooze, which after thousands of years was turned into stone. The glaciers came, then they melted again, at least for a while: primeval forest grew over the land, the apes came, human beings, the Greeks and the Chinese, at least for a while . . . Do you see how beautiful it is? Only its shape has remained.

MARIA: I think it was a snail.

BENJAMIN: It may have been.

MARIA: You haven't even seen a snail, my child!

BENJAMIN: You have a child?

MARIA: Yes, he's dead.

BENJAMIN: Did we kill him?

MARIA: You?

BENJAMIN: Perhaps we killed him.

MARIA: They said it was simply the blast . . . I wanted to get out into the forest, out into the street. I was carrying the child in my arms, the street was on fire. And all of a sudden he was torn out of my arms, that was all I could see.

BENJAMIN: Perhaps we killed him.

MARIA: Why are you looking at me like that?

BENJAMIN: We might have loved each other . . . I've never known a girl.

MARIA: Never?

BENJAMIN: Oh, I've seen plenty of girls I liked looking at when they got into the same tram as me, or hung about in front of the same shop window, perhaps for my benefit. That's true. And I've often been out walking as I'm doing now; I know the spring very well, but alone. You see so much when you wander about alone, you hear so much —

MARIA: Oh yes.

BENJAMIN: The brooks.

MARIA: Oh yes.

BENJAMIN: And there was always such a feeling of expectancy round everything . . . I've often sat like this, just like this, smoking a pipe like a grown-up and thinking all sorts of things. When you lie on your back, with your hands under your head, and the clouds drift by up above — sometimes I used to walk a very long way, on and on, across country, on and on, and then, when it's spring, you tramp through the woods, between the trunks there is nothing but the sky, the blue of the sky, and the wind; have you ever felt that?

MARIA: What?

BENJAMIN: And there was always such a feeling of expectancy round everything . . . especially in the spring . . .

MARIA: I've felt that.

BENJAMIN: I've never sat with a girl as I'm sitting now; as soon as I left school the war broke out and I became an airman —

(He looks at the fossil he has found)

I think we could have loved each other.

(Herbert, a Soldier and the Teacher appear. The Teacher is blindfolded)

HERBERT: Here we are.

SOLDIER: Any special procedure?

HERBERT: You will shoot the prisoner in the chest.

SOLDIER: Common treason —

HERBERT: Fire at the word of command.

(The Soldier moves away)

HERBERT: Be clear about the following:

TEACHER: That I'm going to be shot. I know.

HERBERT: Be clear about the following: If you cry out no one will hear.

TEACHER: I shan't cry out.

HERBERT: If you maintain an exemplary bearing, it will do you no credit; because no one will see.

TEACHER: Shoot!

HERBERT: You will be shot when I give the order.

TEACHER: What more do you want? I have signed letters blindfolded; what more do you want?

HERBERT: I want you to know what you signed blindfolded, that's all.

TEACHER: I don't want to know.

HERBERT: You shall know, whether you want to or not.

TEACHER: Shoot! . . .

HERBERT: Teacher! Sir!

(The Teacher turns his blindfolded head)

TEACHER: Who is it talking to me like that?

HERBERT: Be clear about the following: You are not standing in a famous painting that is shown to school children, there is no gold background behind you — only a grave in the gravel without any hope of being seen.

TEACHER: Who is it talking to me like that?

HERBERT: Be clear about the following: No one will know about your death, no one will paint it on canvas, it will not be admired in any gallery, you will not die according to the laws of beauty, with a foreground, middle distance and background —

TEACHER: Why are you telling me all this?

HERBERT: Why?

TEACHER: At this moment — why?

HERBERT: Be clear about the following: At the same instant as you are shot — the peasants will be scattering manure, the birds singing, the soldiers eating from their mess tins and cracking dirty jokes, a statesman speaking on the radio, I myself shall be smoking a cigarette, another man sitting in the sun fishing, girls will be dancing, others knitting, others washing up, butterflies will be fluttering over the meadow, trains will travel on without the least jolt, people will be sitting at a concert, they will clap in tumultuous applause — your death, Teacher, is a matter of no importance whatever: it will not even be noticed in the picture of reality . . .

NOW THEY'RE SINGING AGAIN

TEACHER: Where have you met me before?

HERBERT: At school, Teacher.

TEACHER: Who are you?

HERBERT: You might have known me. You had time enough. You didn't want to know people, I'm aware of that. You call it humanism —

TEACHER: In God's name, who are you?

HERBERT: Your pupil.

(He goes up to him)

I shall remove your blindfold, so that you can see for yourself who I am.

(He tears off the blindfold)

SOLDIER: Herbert — ?

HERBERT: Don't doubt for a moment that you will be shot.

TEACHER: Herbert — is it you?

HERBERT: I'm showing you what you never showed us: reality, the void, nothingness —

TEACHER: I don't understand.

HERBERT: That's why you're here.

TEACHER: Why?

HERBERT: Your execution will be complete. We shall not merely shoot you, but your words, your thoughts, everything you describe as spirit, your dreams, your aims, your view of the world, which, as you see, was a lie —

(He turns round)

Load!

(To the Teacher again)

If all those things you taught us were true, all that humanism and so on, how could I, your best pupil, now stand before you like this and have you, my teacher, shot like a tethered beast?

TEACHER: It may be that I didn't know myself how true were the things I taught for a lifetime, that I myself didn't entirely believe what I said —

HERBERT: Yes, that's possible.

TEACHER: This is the work of Providence, I can see that; it is no coincidence that it is you, Herbert, who are carrying out this crime against me —

HERBERT: No, it's not coincidence.

TEACHER: I often used to speak of Providence; now I believe in it for the first time!

HERBERT: It isn't Providence either.

TEACHER: What is it then?

HERBERT: I volunteered for the task.

TEACHER: You?

HERBERT: I.

TEACHER: Why?

HERBERT: Why? . . . Remember the morning when we came into the staff room to discuss the freedom of the spirit you had been teaching us about. We brought the textbook and told you: we don't want to learn about so and so and so and so. We threatened you. We tore out the pages that contradicted us, before your eyes. And what did you do?

TEACHER: I couldn't put up a fight.

HERBERT: What did you do?

TEACHER: I had a family — in those days.

HERBERT: What came to light then you call family, but we call it cowardice. You admired courage in the verses of our poets — yes, and it was I myself who started the whole silly business; I wanted to show my schoolfellows the meaning of the word spirit, which they didn't possess and which they therefore called a fraud, stupid as they were. And what happened? The spirit gave way, we tapped it and it was hollow. That was my disillusionment! My schoolfellows were right, stupid as they were; it was a fraud, what we had been taught.

TEACHER: And that's why we're here?

HERBERT: That's the only thing I believe at this moment, and shall believe afterwards, when you lie on this ground —

TEACHER: What?

HERBERT: The criminal, as you call me, is closer to the spirit, he challenges it by force, he is closer to it than the teacher who talks about the spirit, and lies . . . That's all I wanted to say to you.

TEACHER: That's all —

HERBERT: I shall kill, until the spirit comes out from its darkness, if it exists, and until the spirit overcomes me. People will curse us, yes, the whole world will curse us, for centuries. But it is we who will have forced the real spirit to come to light — unless the world perishes with us, because the spirit, the unconquerable spirit, doesn't exist.

(He turns round)

Take aim.

(He walks away)

TEACHER: That's all. Herbert was my best pupil . . .

(Voice from a distance)

HERBERT: Fire!

(Silence)

TEACHER: Now they have fired.

(Voice from a distance)

HERBERT: Follow me. Quick march!

TEACHER: Now they can't hear me any more . . .

(He stands unchanged)

BENJAMIN: I think he can see us. I'll ask him if he will come with us.

TEACHER: Can you tell me where we are?

BENJAMIN: Come with us. There's a monastery, the ruins of a shelled monastery; we're all baking bread together there —

TEACHER: Who?

MARIA: You often said they were devils; you just wanted to see them once, face to face.

LAST SCENE

In the brightly lit foreground appear the survivors: Edward as an officer, Thomas, who is carrying a wreath. Jenny in a black veil, and her two children, of whom the elder is a boy.

JENNY: So this is where they're buried?

EDWARD: Their death was not in vain.

JENNY: On the last evening we saw each other, he was so depressed. I don't know why. He was so depressed . . .

EDWARD: Don't think about that now, Jenny dear!

JENNY: If he knew that our house too is in ruins! Our beautiful big house; people always used to stop and look at it — they used to say it was the finest house in our town. It meant everything to him.

EDWARD: We'll rebuild it, Jenny.

JENNY: Just as it was?

EDWARD: Just as it was —

(To Thomas, who is carrying the wreath)

You shake your head?

THOMAS: It's a great pity our Flight-Lieutenant was lost. We ought to have him here as he was at the last, now that there's going to be peace. He would build differently. It's a great pity.

EDWARD: Give me the wreath —

THOMAS: People say there are hostages buried here too. Twenty-one people from the village. They say the hostages sang as they were shot —

JENNY: Sang?

THOMAS: Do you know what the local people say? Now they're singing again. Whenever they hear shooting, or when any other injustice is done, they say: Now they're singing again!

(The song of the hostages is heard)

They say there were twenty-one of them . . .

(Behind the survivors, who are listening, appears the table of the dead: the twenty-one hostages, sitting in a row holding their bread in their hands, with their mouths closed. Also the Priest, who is feeding them, the dead airmen, Maria, the Teacher, Benjamin, and Karl, who is still kneeling in front of the hostages, his hand over his eyes. But the living cannot see what is happening behind them)

EDWARD: Comrades! If you could only know: the war is over! The war is over, victory is ours —

FLIGHT-LIEUTENANT: That's Jenny, my wife. That's Jenny with the children. That's how they go out in the street, Jenny in black —

THE BOY: Mummy, why are you crying?

JENNY: Your father is here, child, your father is here!

THE BOY: I can't see him.

JENNY: We shall never be able to see him again —

(Jenny weeps silently; the Flight-Lieutenant goes up behind her)

FLIGHT-LIEUTENANT: Jenny, just one word before you go on.

NOW THEY'RE SINGING AGAIN

JENNY: Oh God, oh God!

FLIGHT-LIEUTENANT: We should have lived differently, Jenny. We could have done.

JENNY: Where are the flowers, child, where are the flowers?

THE BOY: They're all wet, Mummy —

FLIGHT-LIEUTENANT: Don't ever rebuild our house, Jenny!

JENNY: Such lovely flowers . . .

FLIGHT-LIEUTENANT: Can you hear me, Jenny?

JENNY: Now lay them down . . .

THE BOY: Where, Mummy?

FLIGHT-LIEUTENANT: Don't ever rebuild our house, Jenny! We weren't happy in it, never. We could have been —

(The Boy's flowers are lying on the ground)

JENNY: How pleased your father would be if he could see your lovely flowers! If he could see how sweet you are —

THE BOY: You gave them to me, Mummy.

JENNY: You must grow up to be a man like him —

FLIGHT-LIEUTENANT: Jenny!

JENNY: You were always his secret pride —

FLIGHT-LIEUTENANT: Can't you hear me, Jenny?

JENNY: All the fine, honourable things your father strove for during his life —

FLIGHT-LIEUTENANT: They were a mistake, Jenny, most of them!

JENNY: You, his son, will carry them on!

FLIGHT-LIEUTENANT: Jenny —

THE BOY: Mummy, you're crying again!

(Jenny covers her face and turns away)

FLIGHT-LIEUTENANT: She can't hear me, Little Father. You tell them! Tell him to shear sheep and not to be my heir. You tell them: Let no one be prevented from becoming better than the others; but let no one be better off than the others before he is a better man.

PRIEST: They can't hear.

FLIGHT-LIEUTENANT: Shout it at them!

PRIEST: They will hear it one day, when they have died.

(Edward lays down the wreath)

RADIO OPERATOR: Now they're laying down the wreath! So that they shall feel better when they leave. And the ribbon too; that's right, so that God can read it.

EDWARD: Comrades, the hour of your mute accusation has come. All that must and will be avenged. You were right! There can be no peace with Satan . . . I hadn't lost my father and my brother then. They're devils; you were right!

RADIO OPERATOR: Edward —

EDWARD: Comrades! . . .

RADIO OPERATOR: He thinks that now we understand each other.

EDWARD: Whatever we do in the future will be done in your name! The judge's sword rests in your hand! The hour of your mute accusation has come; it will not be ignored.

(Edward puts an officer's dagger down with the wreath)

NOW THEY'RE SINGING AGAIN

RADIO OPERATOR: We're not accusing, Edward, that's not true. We're looking for the life we could have lived together. That's all. Did we find it while we were alive?

EDWARD: In this spirit, comrades, we leave your grave but not your memory; your death was not in vain.

FLIGHT-LIEUTENANT: It was in vain.

EDWARD: We pledge ourselves to that.

FLIGHT-LIEUTENANT: It was in vain . . .

(Edward steps back from the wreath, visibly relieved; he puts his cap back on again)

RADIO OPERATOR: Little Father — they make of our death what they please, what suits them. They take the words out of our lives, they make a legacy of them, as they call it, and don't allow us to become more mature than they are themselves.

(Edward has offered Jenny his arm; the tone is now different)

EDWARD: Shall we go?

JENNY: *(sighs)* Ah yes . . .

EDWARD: Before dusk falls.

JENNY: My only consolation is that we shall rebuild everything just as it was —

EDWARD: Just as it was.

THOMAS: Unfortunately . . .

EDWARD: Let's go and have something to eat. We've got time.

(They walk away, leaving the flowers lying on the ground)

FLIGHT-LIEUTENANT: It was in vain.

PRIEST: Don't grieve, Flight-Lieutenant. We'll bake a lot of bread. Everything is in vain, death, life, the stars in the sky, they too are in vain. What else could they be?

BENJAMIN: And love?

PRIEST: Love is beautiful.

BENJAMIN: Tell us, Little Father, is love also in vain?

PRIEST: Love is beautiful, Benjamin, above all else. Love alone knows that it is in vain and love alone does not despair.

(He passes the jug to the man next to him; the song grows louder)

RIP VAN WINKLE

A Radio Play

This is the sketch of a man who never lived because he demanded of himself that he should be the way that others demanded he should be. And one day, when he awoke from this nightmare, lo and behold, people knew his name, it was an esteemed name, and people couldn't tolerate him repudiating that name. They put him in prison, they condemned him to be what he had been and wouldn't tolerate his transformation.

CHARACTERS:

The Stranger • The Public Prosecutor • The Defence Counsel • Julika • Knobel, the prison warder • A Gentleman • A Customs Officer • An Inspector • A Secretary • A Waiter • A Voice on the Telephone • A Newspaper Seller • A Lady • Male Hawker • Female Hawker • A Guard • Voice on the Loudspeaker • Typist • Georges • A Guest • Public at the Railway Station • Customers in the Coffeeshop • Ferstel • The Other • Voice (different from Loudspeaker)

SCENE 1

In a railway station. Whistles are heard in the distance, the steaming of a waiting locomotive, shouts of all kinds, a babble of voices, then above everything the sound of a railwayman going from wheel to wheel testing each one with a hammer.

THE LADY: What's that for?

GENTLEMAN: He's testing to see that all the wheels are sound; they always do that. When will you be in Rome?

LADY: Around midday —

(A guard goes along the train slamming the doors)

GUARD: Take your seats, please. Take your seats, please.

GENTLEMAN: Well then — goodbye.

LADY: Dearest!

GUARD: Take your seats, please.

LADY: But you'll definitely come for Easter —

GENTLEMAN: As soon as I can make it.

GUARD: Take your seats, please. Take your seats, please.

(The guard slams the doors and walks on)

STRANGER: A joke's a joke, but this has gone too far. My train will be leaving at any moment.

CUSTOMS OFFICER: But without you.

STRANGER: This has gone too far.

CUSTOMS OFFICER: You're coming with me.

MALE HAWKER: Hot dogs! Hamburgers!

FEMALE HAWKER: Magazines, cigarettes, magazines!

MALE HAWKER: Hot dogs!

CUSTOMS OFFICER: Come along.

STRANGER: What business is it of yours what my name is? Of course I've got a name, but what business —

CUSTOMS OFFICER: I'm only doing my duty. You know perfectly well that every traveller has to furnish proof of identity.

STRANGER: Why?

CUSTOMS OFFICER: Come with me to the customs office, sir, but get a move on; we'll soon find out who you are.

STRANGER: Take your hands off me!

CUSTOMS OFFICER: It's not my fault if you can't continue your journey.

LOUDSPEAKER: Attention please.

GUARD: Close the doors, please.

LOUDSPEAKER: Copenhagen-Rome Express, departure 11:17. Close the doors, please.

LADY: Goodbye, dearest! Goodbye!

GENTLEMAN: Goodbye.

LADY: See you soon.

MALE HAWKER: Hot dogs! Hamburgers!

FEMALE HAWKER: Cigarettes, magazines, cigarettes!

MALE HAWKER: Hot dogs!

STRANGER: Take your hands off me, I said. That's something I can't stand. Do you hear me? Or I shall give you such a slap in the face your beautiful cap will roll right across the platform.

CUSTOMS OFFICER: You'd better not.

STRANGER: Take that —

(Sound of a slap)

CUSTOMS OFFICER: Good God!

(The train is now whistling, shouts of goodbye against a background of wheels turning faster and faster on the rails)

STRANGER: Here, officer, here's your cap . . .

(Whistle of the locomotive in the distance)

SCENE 2

In an office, the only sound is the ticking of a clock.

INSPECTOR: Take a seat, please.

GENTLEMAN: I don't wish to become involved, Inspector.

INSPECTOR: Sit down, please, sir.

(The gentleman sits down)

Well then, you were standing on the platform and you saw the blow struck. You were saying goodbye to your wife, you say, and it happened outside the same compartment?

GENTLEMAN: Yes.

INSPECTOR: A sleeping compartment.

GENTLEMAN: Mr. Wadel simply refused to give his name, and then the customs officer took him by the sleeve, a moment or two afterwards I heard the slap and saw the cap rolling across the platform.

(The sound of a typewriter)

Is all this being written down?

INSPECTOR: Why not?

GENTLEMAN: Well — the lady I was saying goodbye to wasn't my wife.

INSPECTOR: That makes no difference.

GENTLEMAN: It will to my wife.

INSPECTOR: *(to the typist)* The important thing is the blow, miss, you can leave out all the rest.

GENTLEMAN: Anatol Wadel is a man of temperament, everyone knows that. These artists!

INSPECTOR: You mean you know this gentleman?

GENTLEMAN: Not to speak to, but Anatol Wadel was well known by sight.

INSPECTOR: Very interesting.

GENTLEMAN: I might be mistaken, but he certainly looks very much like him. A few years ago his picture was in all the papers. Don't you remember, Inspector, there was that extraordinary business of his sudden disappearance? No one ever found out where he has been living since then. If he's still alive at all. A fantastic business.

INSPECTOR: Very interesting. You see, the gentleman refuses to give his name, and you call him Anatol Wadel.

GENTLEMAN: I can't swear to it, of course.

(A knock at the door)

His wife lives in Paris, I believe. Julika, her name is.

INSPECTOR: In Paris?

GENTLEMAN: She's a dancer. An enchanting woman.

INSPECTOR: Julika?

GENTLEMAN: Yes.

INSPECTOR: And she is his legal wife?

GENTLEMAN: Definitely.

INSPECTOR: How do you know all this?

GENTLEMAN: From the illustrated papers.

INSPECTOR: Yes, come in.

(The door opens, the Stranger enters)

Thank you, sir. Should it prove necessary, the criminal investigation department will get in touch with you by telephone.

GENTLEMAN: I'd rather they didn't.

INSPECTOR: For today, as I have said, that will be all. Thank you very much for your help.

GENTLEMAN: Good night, gentlemen.

INSPECTOR: Good night, sir.

(The Gentleman goes out, the door is shut behind him)

So you are the gentleman who slapped the customs officer's face?

STRANGER: I am.

INSPECTOR: Please take a seat.

STRANGER: What do you want with me?

INSPECTOR: Take a seat. I see you're pretty drunk still, Mr. Wadel.

STRANGER: My name is not Wadel!

INSPECTOR: But I hope you're able to understand what I'm saying to you.

STRANGER: Inspector, I refuse to allow myself to be pulled by the sleeve. I can't stand it, quite apart from the faces these bullies protected by the law have; I can't stand it, I'm sorry. Of course, I'm quite prepared to pay the usual fine for striking an official.

INSPECTOR: I'm afraid it's not as simple as that.

STRANGER: What's the rate?

INSPECTOR: Please sit down.

STRANGER: I've no time to sit down, Inspector. Thank you very much. I want to catch the next train that will take me out of this intolerable country, never mind in what direction; it doesn't have to be Rome, that was just a whim of mine.

INSPECTOR: You will not leave this room, Mr. Wadel, until we are in possession of your full personal particulars.

STRANGER: Well, for a start my name isn't Wadel.

INSPECTOR: What is it, then? *(The Stranger says nothing)* It is my duty to warn you, Mr. Wadel —

STRANGER: For the last time — my name isn't Wadel.

INSPECTOR: I must warn you that I shall be obliged to get in touch with the criminal investigation department if you continue to refuse to give your name. That would mean your being sent to a remand prison tonight. Have no illusions about that. I shall give you five minutes, sir . . .

(The clock is heard ticking)

SCENE 3

The studio of a ballet school. A piano is playing and a dancing mistress is calling out instructions in French. In between there is hand clapping and the scraping of ballet shoes on the floor.

GEORGES: Julika! Julika!

JULIKA: *(It does not matter if she speaks French with a foreign accent, this is appropriate to the part)* Qu'est-ce qu'il y a?

GEORGES: Telephone.

JULIKA: Je travaille. *(She gives further instructions)*

GEORGES: *(Comes up close to her)* It's urgent.

JULIKA: Why?

GEORGES: It's from abroad.

JULIKA: Who is it?

GEORGES: The police. I think it's about your husband —

JULIKA: M'excusez, Messieurs, dames, je reviendrai tout de suite. Continuez votre exercice, s'il vous plaît.

(The pianist begins playing again, the same tempo as before. Julika goes into a telephone box, where the sound of the ballet shoes is heard muted)

Hello? — Julika. — I beg your pardon? — Yes, this is Julika Wadel speaking. — Criminal investigation department? — I know nothing whatever. — My husband? No, I've no idea at all. — Of course. — I understand. As soon as I can, of course, but I can't leave on the spur of the moment, Inspector; I run a ballet school, you know. — Five years ago, that's right. He disappeared exactly five years ago last February. — As soon as I can, Inspector, of course I shall recognize my husband. — Thank you for letting me know. — Not at all.

(Julika hangs up. She breathes audibly. Leaves the phone box, so that the music is heard louder again)

GEORGES: What's happened.

JULIKA: My husband —

GEORGES: You're as white as a sheet, Julika.

JULIKA: They say my husband has turned up again.

GEORGES: What of it?

JULIKA: They arrested him at the border, they say. I'm to go over there at once.

GEORGES: What for?

JULIKA: I always thought that would happen — one fine day. All of a sudden, there he is again.

GEORGES: What does it matter to you? For five years he didn't bother about you, Julika. I thought you were through with him.

JULIKA: So I am.

GEORGES: A man who has messed up half your life, you always say so yourself, and now —

JULIKA: Oh Georges!

GEORGES: Are you going?

JULIKA: We'll see.

(The music has meanwhile fallen silent. Julika claps her hands)

Messieurs, dames, nous continuons.

(Music as at the beginning)

SCENE 4

A cell in the remand prison.

DEFENCE COUNSEL: Allow me to introduce myself. My name is Dünner, Hans Ulrich Dünner, lawyer. I have had the honour, Mr. Wadel, of being appointed by the court to defend you.

STRANGER: My name is not Wadel.

COUNSEL: You may rest assured that I shall do everything in my power, and there is no cause for despondency. I have studied the brief, and if you will have the goodness to tell me, at least in broad outline, where you have spent the last five years, I am quite sure that in a few days you will be a free man again.

STRANGER: H'm.

COUNSEL: May I sit down?

(Counsel sits down on the bed)

I know these prison beds are rather hard. But clean. Incidentally, I took immediate steps to see that your stay in the remand prison, which I hope will only last a few days, shall be as comfortable as possible. You have the best cell in the building, the only one that gets the morning sun and has a view of the old plane trees; you hear almost no noise from the street here — only the cooing of the pigeons.

STRANGER: And the bells of your cathedral!

COUNSEL: Don't you like them?

STRANGER: They're enough to drive one mad.

COUNSEL: They're supposed to be the finest chimes in our whole country.

STRANGER: What do I care about your country?

COUNSEL: Even if they do boom a bit when you're so close. I'm sorry our remand prison is just opposite the cathedral; I'm afraid that is something we can't change. To keep to the point, Mr. Wadel: allow me to ask —

STRANGER: Good God, man, my name isn't Wadel. How often do I have to tell you?

COUNSEL: Where have you been for the last five years?

STRANGER: I told the warder I wouldn't see anyone until I'd had my whisky. What a way to carry on! Last night I threw them out; today they sneak into my cell while I'm asleep. I must say —

COUNSEL: It's past ten.

STRANGER: Have you any whisky, or haven't you?

(The counsel puts a file down on the table)

A whole file? For a single slap in the face? I've only been in your country three days, are you telling me this whole file . . .

COUNSEL: Trivialities. Don't worry. They're nothing but trivialities: fleeing the country without notifying the authorities, tax evasion, endangering traffic by leaving a hedge uncut for several years in spite of six warnings, non-compliance with air defence regulations, ignoring all official communications, non-payment of old age insurance — and so on, Mr. Wadel, and so on.

STRANGER: For the last time: my name is not Wadel!!! *(A brief silence)* What is all this about? I've just come from Mexico and I must say the human sacrifices of the Aztecs, who used to cut the living heart out of their victims' bodies, were child's play compared with the treatment meted out in this country to a living man who has no papers, or no wish to show them. What business is it of yours who I am? You have mislaid a citizen, a certain Mr. Wadel. What can I do about that? — And now you think I'm going to let myself be persuaded I'm the missing man? Me! That's what you want. You think you can torture me till I lose my reason and start believing that I really am the man you're looking for.

COUNSEL: Who is talking about torture?

STRANGER: Don't you think it's torture to look at you, Mr. Dünner, with your innocent expression? What earthly right have you to sit on my bed, looking through a file that has absolutely nothing to do with me? . . . *(Yells)* What do you want anyway?

COUNSEL: I want to defend you —

STRANGER: *(Laughs)*

COUNSEL: I have been told that you are Mr. Wadel, Anatol Wadel, the sculptor, who disappeared five years ago, and I have accepted the task —

STRANGER: Of defending Anatol Wadel.

COUNSEL: Yes.

STRANGER: But I tell you I'm not he.

COUNSEL: Why aren't you?

STRANGER: Because I'm not.

COUNSEL: Anatol Wadel is very highly thought of. The Academy has already informed me that they are prepared not only to pay your fine for slapping the customs officer's face, but also to meet any other expenses you may have incurred. I really don't understand you: why do you refuse to be Anatol Wadel?

STRANGER: Because I'm not Anatol Wadel.

COUNSEL: H'm.

STRANGER: I'm sorry.

(The counsel falls silent: the cathedral clock booms out the hour)

SCENE 5

In the café. Muted background music, jazz on a piano, at intervals the hiss of an espresso machine, voices.

GENTLEMAN: Waiter!

WAITER: Just a moment, sir.

GENTLEMAN: I'm afraid I must go, my wife is waiting for me.

THE OTHER: How is she?

GENTLEMAN: Oh, under the weather again. Unfortunately. I really wanted to go to Rome over Easter. Couldn't be done. I already had the plane tickets, the hotel was booked and so on . . . Waiter, the bill, please.

WAITER: Very good, sir.

GENTLEMAN: I'm in a hurry.

NEWSPAPER SELLER: Late night final. Sunday sport. Paper . . . The new atomic weapon, sir; the Wadel case.

GENTLEMAN: So it is him. The Wadel case! Didn't I tell you I saw him at the station the other day? Well, it seems I was right.

(The newspaper seller goes on)

NEWSPAPER SELLER: Late night final. Sunday sport. Paper.

RIP VAN WINKLE

(The espresso machine hisses)

THE OTHER: Did you know Wadel, then?

GENTLEMAN: Well, not to speak to; but he used to sit over there in that alcove every evening. Don't you remember? That odd fellow who always drank whisky. Spiteful people said he was afraid to go home.

THE OTHER: Because of his wife?

GENTLEMAN: And yet he had the most enchanting wife you can imagine, as delicate as a dragonfly. It's none of my business. They say she was mortally ill at the time, all because of that Wadel —

WAITER: Sir?

GENTLEMAN: I'd like my bill.

WAITER: Thank you very much, sir.

GENTLEMAN: That's all right.

WAITER: Thank you very much!

GENTLEMAN: She had T.B., I believe.

THE OTHER: And all because of him.

GENTLEMAN: No sooner had he disappeared than she got better, you couldn't believe your eyes, no trace of T.B. any more, she was younger than ever, the personification of radiant health —

THE OTHER: The moment he disappeared.

GENTLEMAN: She blossomed as never before.

(The espresso machine hisses)

THE OTHER: By the way, why aren't you going to Rome after all?

GENTLEMAN: I can't leave my wife, now that she's ill. That's just the trouble. She would — I don't know what she would do if I left her now.

THE OTHER: Who knows? She might blossom as never before.

(The espresso machine hisses)

SCENE 6

In the cell. There is a knock on the door. No answer. The knock is repeated.

STRANGER: Come in.

(The door opens)

Who are you?

(The door is shut)

PUBLIC PROSECUTOR: Allow me to introduce myself. I'm the public prosecutor. Please don't get up.

STRANGER: The bed is wide enough, Mr. Public Prosecutor, sit down.

PROSECUTOR: Do you smoke?

STRANGER: Thank you, yes, I do.

(The Prosecutor gives him a light)

PROSECUTOR: By the way, I've come in an entirely private capacity. Please don't regard this as an interrogation, I simply felt an urge to see you, if you are our esteemed Anatol Wadel.

STRANGER: I'm not.

PROSECUTOR: You see, my wife is a great admirer of your art; she is terribly upset to think that an artist like Anatol Wadel, a man of the spirit, a creator, to whom our city is indebted for such delightful sculptures, should be sitting on this prison bed like a common criminal.

STRANGER: I am a common criminal.

PROSECUTOR: So you say, I know. The warder tells me you claim to have committed at least five murders.

STRANGER: Why don't people believe me?

PROSECUTOR: One of them, I believe, was your esteemed wife.

STRANGER: She was my first murder.

PROSECUTOR: H'm.

STRANGER: A wonderful cigar, Mr. Public Prosecutor.

PROSECUTOR: As I said before, don't look upon it as an interrogation if I permit myself the question: Why did you murder your wife?

STRANGER: I loved her.

PROSECUTOR: Is that a reason?

STRANGER: Besides which she was devastatingly beautiful.

PROSECUTOR: You mean you were jealous of her?

STRANGER: I had no grounds for jealousy. Perhaps she was a bit happier with other men, I don't know, but there certainly wasn't a man in the world who could have made her suffer more deeply than I did. I know that.

PROSECUTOR: You loved her?

STRANGER: What do you mean by love? She sacrificed herself, you know, she was a sufferer. All our friends thought so. You see, it was I who made her ill, mortally ill.

PROSECUTOR: How?

STRANGER: I don't know. With T.B. She said so. That's to say, she didn't actually say so, but everyone knew. It was a sacrifice to live at my side, and yet she forgave me over and over again.

PROSECUTOR: What did she forgive?

STRANGER: Me.

PROSECUTOR: Did you often quarrel?

STRANGER: Never.

PROSECUTOR: That's terrible.

STRANGER: You've said it, Mr. Public Prosecutor. The peace that reigned between us was terrible. When I couldn't stand it any longer and smashed a plate against the wall, I felt for days like a murderer — her murderer.

PROSECUTOR: H'm.

STRANGER: It was unbearable.

PROSECUTOR: And so, as the warder told me, you joined the Foreign Legion.

STRANGER: I'm a coward, yes.

PROSECUTOR: I don't understand that, to be frank —

STRANGER: Nor do I, but that's how it was.

PROSECUTOR: You loved her —

STRANGER: She was an angel.

PROSECUTOR: What was the trouble then?

STRANGER: I couldn't stand always having a bad conscience.

PROSECUTOR: And therefore you murdered her?

STRANGER: I told you. It was terrible for her to live at my side.

PROSECUTOR: When did this murder take place?

STRANGER: Ha.

PROSECUTOR: Why do you laugh?

STRANGER: I must say, Mr. Public Prosecutor, you make things very easy for yourself. You imagine that for a single cigar I shall save you all the work you are paid to do; in fact I don't understand this whole procedure: you ask me to prove myself guilty of the crime for which I am to be condemned, to be a respectable citizen and be called Anatol Wadel, to whom your city, as I hear, is indebted for such delightful sculptures. Mr. Public Prosecutor, I must say —

PROSECUTOR: Go on.

STRANGER: It is a public prosecutor's job to prove that I am a murderer, not mine — at least I have always thought that was the situation in a constitutional state.

PROSECUTOR: Don't misunderstand me.

STRANGER: I'm not Anatol Wadel. How many more times do I have to tell you? And I am not going to let your good wife persuade me I am, no one is indebted to me for delightful sculptures!

PROSECUTOR: My dear sir —

STRANGER: No one.

PROSECUTOR: Don't excite yourself.

STRANGER: Do I have to strangle my defending counsel, merely to prove that I am not the respectable citizen you have lost?

PROSECUTOR: You misunderstand us. Nobody wants to compel you to be someone you aren't, and as soon as you tell us who you really are —

STRANGER: Who I really am!

PROSECUTOR: Why do you shake your head?

STRANGER: For a week, since I was put in this prison, where I am treated as a respectable citizen, I have repeated day after day that I refuse to give any further information without whisky; for without whisky I'm not myself, I know that; without whisky I'm lost, for when I'm sober I'm far too susceptible to all kinds of moral pressure and willing to play a part that has nothing to do with me, nothing at all, I've learnt that from experience. Why don't they bring me any whisky? I've already made the rather helpful suggestion that you can save yourselves the cost of my officially appointed defence counsel and supply me with whisky instead, because there is no sense in my going into the dock without whisky — no sense at all, Mr. Public Prosecutor, you will never be able to recognize my true identity, I can't myself — as long as I'm kept without whisky.

PROSECUTOR: H'm.

STRANGER: That is all I have to say in this sober state.

(The hour booms out from the cathedral)

SCENE 7

On an airfield. The noise of running engines, which is heard now louder now quieter in the waiting hall; in the background a loudspeaker.

LOUDSPEAKER: Attention please, may I have your attention please. Flight number 209, London-Paris-Munich, ready for departure.

JULIKA: That's mine.

LOUDSPEAKER: All passengers are requested to board the plane as soon as possible.

JULIKA: I must go.

LOUDSPEAKER: Attention s'il vous plaît . . .

(Engine roar drowns speaker)

JULIKA: Well, then, dear, goodbye.

GEORGES: As you like.

JULIKA: I must. You will understand.

GEORGES: No.

JULIKA: Georges —

GEORGES: All these years you have been telling me how he made you ill, your Anatol, and no sooner does he pop up again —

JULIKA: I'm coming back, Georges.

GEORGES: We shall see about that, my dear — I think you've got to board the plane.

JULIKA: Perhaps it isn't him at all.

GEORGES: There's no need to cry, Julika, all you need is a man whom you can convince that he's making you ill. Isn't that so? You're only happy when you can feel sorry for yourself.

JULIKA: Georges —

GEORGES: You're a born sufferer.

LOUDSPEAKER: Attention please. British European Airways announce the departure of flight number 209. This is our last call: passenger Mrs. Julika Wadel, please come to the information desk immediately.

GEORGES: Goodbye.

JULIKA: Goodbye.

(The noise of a revving engine drowns everything)

SCENE 8

In the cell. The warder can be heard cleaning, the sounds of floor cloths and a bucket.

KNOBEL: I'll be finished in a minute. I've only got the bars to do.

STRANGER: You're not disturbing me. Carry on cleaning. You're the only person I can bear to have in my cell, Knobel: you believe me.

KNOBEL: If you say yourself you murdered your wife, Mr. van Winkle —

STRANGER: But don't tell anyone my name is Rip van Winkle.

KNOBEL: You know, there are plenty of others in the building who are quite different. When I bring them their grub or clean their cells they all deny having done anything. I can't stand it any more. They're all innocent. For thirteen years I've been a warder. In all that time you are the first, Mr. van Winkle, who has had the kindness to tell me about his murders, and in detail, so that even as a layman I can picture them. The very first. Before that I was a greengrocer. I imagined everything quite differently when I took this job. You'll get to hear some interesting stories, I thought. But not a bit of it. Here I am a warder in a state prison, and when I want to listen to criminals I have to go to the cinema like everyone else.

(He takes the bucket)

That's done.

STRANGER: When will you be coming back?

KNOBEL: As soon as I have time, Mr. van Winkle.

STRANGER: My second murder was in the jungle, that was quite different, by then I knew that I was a murderer, I didn't need to be in any special mood for it, you see; it was a foregone conclusion.

KNOBEL: You were in the jungle?

STRANGER: In Jamaica, yes, of course. I knew Ferstel was knocking around in Jamaica, and it was only a question of patience before he fell under my dagger.

KNOBEL: Who is Ferstel?

STRANGER: The hair oil gangster.

KNOBEL: You never told me about him before.

STRANGER: A millionaire. You know, one of the kind you can't get at in a constitutional state —

(The cathedral clock strikes eleven)

I'll tell you about that another time, my dear Knobel. It's impossible to talk with this din going on.

KNOBEL: In Jamaica, you said?

STRANGER: If this cathedral isn't torture I don't know what is.

KNOBEL: And you did him in with a dagger?

STRANGER: Sure.

KNOBEL: Well I'm damned!

STRANGER: With an Indian dagger . . .

KNOBEL: Well I'm damned.

(A clock strikes eleven. As soon as it finishes the nearby cathedral booms out the time once more)

SCENE 9

The acoustics of a corridor. The chimes die away and fall silent.

COUNSEL: We'll try it, Madame. We shall hear whether he has calmed down.

JULIKA: I must see him.

COUNSEL: As I told you, the chimes always drive him crazy —

JULIKA: He will recognize me.

COUNSEL: I'll go first, Madame.

JULIKA: Please do.

COUNSEL: When we are outside the cell, don't say a word.

(They walk down a long corridor, the echo of their footsteps can be heard — the listener is walking with them — and finally the silence when they stop)

JULIKA: Here?

COUNSEL: Ssh.

(A sudden clatter in the cell)

STRANGER: Who's there?

JULIKA: In heaven's name —

STRANGER: Who's there?

COUNSEL: Ssh.

STRANGER: Whisky! Whisky! Whisky!

JULIKA: What is he shouting?

STRANGER: I want whisky.

COUNSEL: It's no use. We may as well go.

(A fresh clatter in the cell)

JULIKA: Terrible.

STRANGER: I want whisky.

COUNSEL: Come.

STRANGER: I want whisky! I want whisky!

(They move away from the cell)

(Shouts continue:) I want whisky! I want whisky!

(The shouts gradually die away, followed by footsteps passing along the crooked corridor. Silence. A door is opened)

COUNSEL: After you, Madame.

(They enter; the door is closed; inside a room)

PROSECUTOR: Well?

COUNSEL: He hasn't calmed down in the least. No sooner does he hear footsteps than he starts yelling for whisky again. — May I introduce you? The Public Prosecutor.

JULIKA: How do you do.

COUNSEL: Mrs. Wadel, Mrs. Julika Wadel.

PROSECUTOR: Ah.

COUNSEL: Mrs. Wadel arrived yesterday.

PROSECUTOR: How do you do.

COUNSEL: As I feared, Mr. Public Prosecutor, our prisoner refuses to remember having been married. The mere information that a lady had arrived who considers herself his wife made him so furious again that it is impossible to enter his cell.

PROSECUTOR: I see . . . Mrs. Wadel, won't you sit down?

(They sit down)

JULIKA: After so many years, gentlemen, you can't imagine how I felt on suddenly hearing the news that my husband had turned up again. To be frank, I've never heard my husband behaving like that before; that isn't his way, Mr. Public Prosecutor, believe me.

PROSECUTOR: Do you smoke?

JULIKA: Not now. Thank you.

PROSECUTOR: I presume Mr. Dünner has already told you how the arrest was made.

JULIKA: More or less.

PROSECUTOR: Entering the country without papers, refusing to answer questions, striking an official, all this is regrettable, Madame, but no reason not to be heartily glad, if our prisoner really is the missing Anatol Wadel. We all know his name, Madame, and admire his art, even if we can't understand it . . . The charges against the missing Anatol Wadel are known to you: Neglecting all duties, failing to exercise his civil rights, fleeing the country without notifying the authorities. Tax evasion, non-compliance with air defence regulations, failure to report to the police after repeated warnings about the interference to traffic caused by his overgrown garden hedge and so on. Other misdemeanours may possibly have to be taken into account; undermining the morale of our army by serving in the Foreign Legion, for example. But all this, as I said, is no reason, Madame, why you shouldn't be glad he has come back, if you really are his wife.

JULIKA: Who else do you think I am?

PROSECUTOR: Don't misunderstand me.

JULIKA: Am I his wife! My name is Wadel, Julika Wadel, born —

PROSECUTOR: We know that.

JULIKA: Here are my papers, look.

PROSECUTOR: Madame, the point at issue is not whether you are the wife of our missing Anatol Wadel.

JULIKA: What is it then?

PROSECUTOR: Whether our prisoner is the missing Anatol Wadel. You see, he denies it. And up to the present, Madame, we have not succeeded in proving that he is.

JULIKA: He denies it?

COUNSEL: He certainly does!

PROSECUTOR: What may I offer you, Madame?

JULIKA: He denies it . . .

PROSECUTOR: Do you drink whisky?

JULIKA: Whisky?

PROSECUTOR: I'm sure you won't blame me for keeping whisky in my desk, Madame. I simply can't stand it: for a week that man has been yelling for whisky all the time, whisky, whisky, whisky!

(The sound of glasses)

Unfortunately we can't give him any.

(The sound of pouring)

How do you like it, Madame? Half and half?

COUNSEL: As I told you, Mrs. Wadel. The Public Prosecutor entirely agrees with us; we neither of us believe for a moment that your husband is a murderer, no matter how often he swears he is.

JULIKA: A murderer?

COUNSEL: He says so every day.

JULIKA: My husband — ?

PROSECUTOR: He claims to have committed at least five murders.

COUNSEL: Which he can't prove.

PROSECUTOR: Any more than his defence counsel can prove that he didn't commit these murders. Here you are, Madame, your whisky.

JULIKA: Gentlemen, Anatol is not a murderer.

PROSECUTOR: Let us hope not, Madame.

JULIKA: Anatol — he simply wouldn't be capable of it, not a man like Anatol; believe me, I was married to him for eight years!

PROSECUTOR: That's exactly what makes him so wild.

JULIKA: What?

PROSECUTOR: That none of us believes he is a murderer. Your health, Madame, your health. It is indeed an unusual case and one which, as you can see, has come to preoccupy us beyond the limits of our professional duty. We are used to murderers who yell all day long, I am innocent. That doesn't interfere with my work for an instant, and it would never occur to me to drink whisky in the middle of the day on that account. But a man who denies his innocence and practically gets apoplexy when he is suspected of being a respectable citizen, that does get on one's nerves, Madame, believe me. Your husband is turning our whole system upside down, Madame — if he is your husband.

JULIKA: Whom does he claim to have murdered?

PROSECUTOR: You.

JULIKA: Me — ?

PROSECUTOR: For example, yes. Don't be scared.

JULIKA: Murdered — me —

PROSECUTOR: You can understand, Madame, that we are curious to see what sort of a face he makes when he finds himself confronted by you.

JULIKA: In heaven's name —

PROSECUTOR: Your health, Madame.

JULIKA: *(Bursts into tears)*

COUNSEL: Mrs. Wadel —

JULIKA: In heaven's name —

PROSECUTOR: Drink up your whisky, Madame, get a grip on yourself. Surely you're not going to believe that he murdered you — Madame! . . .

JULIKA: *(Sobs uncontrollably)*

SCENE 10

In the cell.

STRANGER: And that was yesterday?

KNOBEL: Yes.

STRANGER: And you told them I was going on a hunger strike?

KNOBEL: Yes.

STRANGER: What's that, Knobel?

KNOBEL: A kind of salami.

STRANGER: Unofficial?

KNOBEL: Of course.

STRANGER: But don't tell them I'm eating just the same —

KNOBEL: Mr. van Winkle, what do you take me for?

STRANGER: Thank you, Knobel, thank you.

(The prisoner eats audibly)

And she sobbed?

KNOBEL: I don't know what she wants.

STRANGER: How does she look?

KNOBEL: Don't worry, Mr. van Winkle. You must eat, to keep your nerves in good trim. She looks smart. Blonde. And she fills the whole corridor with scent.

STRANGER: Blonde?

KNOBEL: Why not?

STRANGER: Has she a figure?

KNOBEL: And how!

STRANGER: It's a dirty trick. A man in my position, a prisoner, who has no choice. How could I help getting carried away, I ask you, when a woman comes along and says: You're the one and only man for me?

KNOBEL: Eat, Mr. van Winkle, perhaps she isn't your type at all, even though she claims to be your wife.

STRANGER: My type —

KNOBEL: Eat! Before someone comes.

STRANGER: Have I told you the story of the little mulatto girl?

KNOBEL: No.

STRANGER: She was my type.

KNOBEL: A mulatto girl?

STRANGER: Haven't you any bread?

KNOBEL: Sorry, Mr. van Winkle.

STRANGER: That was on the Rio Grande . . . My dear Knobel, it's impossible to describe to anyone who hasn't seen it with his own eyes — a sunset in the desert, for example. As far as the eye can see, nothing but desert, brown, yellow, here and there a cactus, otherwise nothing, but a cactus, my dear Knobel, like a seven-branched candlestick and as high as a house.

KNOBEL: Well I'm damned!

STRANGER: Suddenly — we were just squatting round our fire, because the evenings in the desert were bitterly cold, discussing with the smugglers how they were going to get us across the Mexican border during the night, you see there was a warrant out for my arrest already — suddenly he came round the rocks.

KNOBEL: Are there rocks too?

STRANGER: And what rocks, red like fresh bull's blood. In the shadow they are violet. And overhead a starry sky, clear as only a night sky over the desert can be —

KNOBEL: And who came round the rocks? Who was it?

STRANGER: A limousine. Stolen, of course. A banner of golden dust. A limousine speeding straight across the open desert. Pitching like a yawl, up and down over the waves of sand — bang! I fired, but the fellow drove on, and of course I thought it was the police. Bang! Bang! And who do you think was in the car?

KNOBEL: Who?

STRANGER: Jim.

KNOBEL: Who was Jim?

STRANGER: Her husband.

KNOBEL: The mulatto girl's?

STRANGER: Of course.

KNOBEL: Well I'm damned!

STRANGER: A negro. A charming fellow, but not when you'd stolen his wife, of course. Not in the darkness like that, when you could only see his white teeth and his white eyes — cheers!

KNOBEL: What happened then?

STRANGER: You see, we loved each other.

KNOBEL: The mulatto girl and you?

STRANGER: I asked her: Do you love me or do you love him? She understood me perfectly — and nodded . . . And bang. And not another word from Jim.

KNOBEL: He was dead?

STRANGER: On the spot.

KNOBEL: Well I'm damned!

STRANGER: She kissed me. That's my type.

KNOBEL: Well I'm damned!

STRANGER: I like negroes, but I can't stand husbands, even if they're negroes. Watch what you do all the time — that's not my way. Of course we drove straight across the border.

KNOBEL: To Mexico —

STRANGER: Without lights, of course. To the left of the Rio Grande. In the full moon.

KNOBEL: That was your third murder?

STRANGER: I think so . . .

KNOBEL: Have this salami too, Mr. van Winkle. I'm afraid I must move on. The others are always swearing at me for spending so long with you.

STRANGER: Love is based on rape, everything else is poppycock, believe me, poppycock for thin-blooded bourgeois like Mr. Dünner and his sort. When I think how I first saw Florence — in the sawmill . . .

KNOBEL: You mean the mulatto girl?

STRANGER: Way up in California, you know; I had gone down to the seashore to fish, because I had no money to buy any other food. Suddenly — it was midday and not a cloud in the sky — smoke started billowing up from inshore behind me, such clouds of smoke it looked like an eclipse of the sun, suddenly. That can only be the big sawmill, I thought, in this lonely district. You must picture it: for hours on end not a single house, a few sheep, nothing else. Down below the surf with pelicans and barking seals. And as I panted my way up the hill the sky was filled with flying sparks; I've never seen a fire like it. And how the flames roared! Not a trace of a fire engine, naturally. The women were standing howling, biting their fingernails and praying to God to make the wind drop. There was no water to put it out with, and as it was Sunday, the men were away in the distant town. And flames were bursting out of every roof and window, flapping and snapping in the air like purple banners. A magnificent sight. But there was nothing to be done. Outside a whole ocean of wind, and as it blew into those stacks of dry timber it created a heat you couldn't stand at a distance of a hundred paces. And right in the middle stood a tank full of gas . . . I asked her if she was mad, the tank might blow up at any moment, nevertheless she ran into her hut . . .

KNOBEL: Who?

STRANGER: Right in the middle of all the smoke. The young mulatto girl.

KNOBEL: Well I'm damned!

STRANGER: And I — ran after her!

KNOBEL: Naturally.

STRANGER: What do you mean, naturally? It was utter madness, but I thought, perhaps she is trying to save a child. — Anyhow, there I stood in the hut, a few of the shingles were already on fire, an old negro was running about on the roof with a ridiculous garden hose, trying to pour water on the burning shingles, one at a time, and inside there was so much smoke it was almost suffocating. Hello, I yelled. What can I rescue? And there she stood, motionless, crying, her hands on her hips, a young mulatto girl, and what a girl, Knobel! Everything else in there was rubbish, not worth saving; I was so furious I just grabbed hold of her and shook her.

KNOBEL: Why?

STRANGER: She wanted me to save the fridge. Like hell I will, I yelled. And up on the roof the old negro was still squirting the shingles with his thin garden hose. What do you want? she said. You, I said. And when I grabbed her she laughed with every tooth in her head. I've got a husband! she said. Come on, I said. Have you got a car? she asked. There are plenty of cars about, I said. And when I put my arms around her the roof was already crackling so that the sparks flew. I carried her to the first car standing in the road, shoved her in and drove off. The owner, a tourist, didn't even notice as I shot past him; everyone was watching the gas tank that was liable to blow up at any moment.

KNOBEL: And you made off?

STRANGER: Four hours later we were sitting fishing behind a rock, where no one could see us.

KNOBEL: Well I'm damned!

STRANGER: What's your name? I asked. Florence, she said. My husband will kill you if he catches us. I merely laughed and she broke open the shellfish for bait.

(A knock at the door)

Ssh.

KNOBEL: Did you catch anything?

STRANGER: This biiiig —

KNOBEL: Well I'm damned!

(A knock at the door)

STRANGER: Come in.

(The door opens)

KNOBEL: Good morning, sir.

(The warder goes out, shutting the door behind him)

STRANGER: Why so dejected, Mr. Dünner?

COUNSEL: Good morning.

STRANGER: Take a seat.

COUNSEL: You've been lying to me.

STRANGER: What's that album for?

COUNSEL: You told me you couldn't remember being married or even having lived in our city; in fact you said you couldn't imagine life in our city at all.

STRANGER: Not without whisky.

COUNSEL: Then what about this album? Just look at it. Why do you lie? Here it is in black and white: Anatol in his first studio, Anatol on the beach at Saintes-Maries — I suppose you don't remember this blonde lady either? Here: Anatol on the Eiffel Tower. Anatol smoking a pipe, Anatol by the Russian memorial in Berlin. And look here, in black and white: you sitting at the table beside our mayor, who has just made a speech about you and is shaking your hand. And so on. Why do you deny being this man?

STRANGER: Where did you get this album?

COUNSEL: Do you think you can make a fool of me —

STRANGER: I asked you where you got this album.

COUNSEL: Here, look, you feeding the swans, none other than you. And in the background, you can see for yourself, the cathedral, our cathedral! And for a week you've been telling me — me your defending counsel — that you never lived in our city.

STRANGER: What do you mean by "lived"?

COUNSEL: I got the album from the lady who will come to visit you this morning.

STRANGER: Maybe I did feed swans. With your impossible cathedral in the background, in black and white; but to have fed swans and sat beside your mayor doesn't prove that I — lived here.

COUNSEL: Where did you live then?

STRANGER: Certainly not here, not in this album.

COUNSEL: You can tell our warder that you've been in the jungle, but not me. In ten days we shall have to go into the dock, and what sort of figure shall I cut, your officially appointed defence counsel, what sort of figure shall I cut?

STRANGER: That's your affair, Mr. Dünner.

COUNSEL: I'm doing all I can!

STRANGER: I feel sorry for you, Mr. Dünner.

COUNSEL: Why are you so stubborn? When I tell you our city is actually prepared to award you a prize of money that will enable you to pay off your outstanding taxes immediately. In fact why this obstinacy, when you're got everything: a studio, a famous name, a wife who is ready to sacrifice herself for you —

STRANGER: That's the last straw.

COUNSEL: The Academy is prepared to pay the fine for striking an official, and almost everyone who meets you in the streets will be glad you're back, even your old enemies. Why do you refuse to be our esteemed Anatol Wadel?

STRANGER: My dear Mr. Dünner —

COUNSEL: Why?

STRANGER: Because I'm not Anatol Wadel. As for this lady, as I said, I have nothing against visits from ladies, but I can only repeat my warning. I'm a very sensual man, especially in the spring. Utterly uninhibited.

COUNSEL: I told her.

STRANGER: And this lady insists on meeting me in this cell?

COUNSEL: Absolutely.

STRANGER: Just the two of us?

COUNSEL: She says she can scarcely wait to talk to you. She is convinced that you are her husband. She says —

STRANGER: What?

COUNSEL: She burst out sobbing when she heard about your supposed murder. She said she knew her husband better than he knew himself. And any talk of uninhibited passion, says the lady, is a lot of nonsense. She says that was always a fantasy of her husband's, and she is quite sure she can manage you on her own.

STRANGER: If she thinks so.

COUNSEL: I don't understand you. One word admitting that you are the missing man, and tomorrow you would be free.

STRANGER: Free!

COUNSEL: Why do you laugh?

STRANGER: As Wadel, Anatol Wadel, citizen of this city, to which he has given so many delightful sculptures — Mr. Dünner, it's hopeless. Why don't you go for a walk?

COUNSEL: What is hopeless?

STRANGER: Your whole line of defence.

COUNSEL: Why?

STRANGER: Let's talk about Russia.

COUNSEL: I really don't understand you, Mr. Wadel —

STRANGER: *(Yells)* My name isn't Wadel!!!

(A brief silence)

COUNSEL: What is it then? I ask you. What is it then?

(A knock at the door)

If you don't tell me some name, how am I to defend you — a man without a name?

STRANGER: That's just the point.

(Another knock)

COUNSEL: Come in.

(The door opens)

What is it, Knobel?

KNOBEL: The lady.

COUNSEL: Ah.

STRANGER: Ask her to come in.

(The lady enters the cell)

JULIKA: Anatol. *(Silence)* Anatol, don't you recognize me?

STRANGER: Please take a seat, Madame.

COUNSEL: If you don't mind, Mrs. Wadel, I shall leave now. As I told you, the cell door will be locked, but the warder is always somewhere near, he will hear if anyone calls.

(The counsel and the warder — and with them the listener — leave the cell. Outside in the corridor)

Knobel, stay nearby.

KNOBEL: Of course.

COUNSEL: Just in case.

KNOBEL: Don't worry.

(The counsel walks away down the corridor)

SCENE 11

In the public prosecutor's office.

PROSECUTOR: I don't know, Counsellor, I don't know. Perhaps there's another way of looking at the matter.

COUNSEL: Not for me, Public Prosecutor.

PROSECUTOR: You ask this man to tell you the whole truth, the truth about where and how he has been living —

COUNSEL: I'm his defence counsel.

PROSECUTOR: What is truth?

COUNSEL: Really, Public Prosecutor — the album and all the rest, evidence upon evidence, to say nothing of the fact that the lady, Mrs. Wadel, recognized him immediately — now they've been together in his cell for an hour.

PROSECUTOR: What of that?

COUNSEL: There's no doubt that he is her husband.

PROSECUTOR: H'm.

COUNSEL: Why do you smile?

PROSECUTOR: I'll tell you something, Counsellor. I've been a public prosecutor for more than twenty years. I know only one thing: that everything can be proved, except truth. Believe me, no one, even under torture, is capable of telling the truth, unless he invents it.

COUNSEL: Do you believe in his Wild West stories?

PROSECUTOR: In a certain sense, yes.

COUNSEL: Joking apart, Public Prosecutor —

PROSECUTOR: If you only believe a man when he tells you the acts he has really performed, my dear Dünner, you will never get to know him. You and your demand for the whole truth! As though the thousand pictures we fear or hope for, and all the acts that remain unperformed in our lives, were not also part of the truth of our lives . . .

(A knock at the door)

Come in.

(The warder enters)

KNOBEL: The lady would like to speak to you.

COUNSEL: Where is she?

KNOBEL: She will be here in a minute, Mr. Dünner, as soon as she has combed her hair.

PROSECUTOR: Combed her hair?

KNOBEL: She has everything in her handbag, powder and lipstick. The lady has lost a button, she says.

PROSECUTOR: A button?

KNOBEL: That's what she said. From her skirt.

PROSECUTOR: What happened, Knobel?

KNOBEL: I don't know, sir. I was in the corridor, I didn't hear anything —

(The lady enters)

PROSECUTOR: Take a seat, Mrs. Wadel.

JULIKA: Thank you . . .

PROSECUTOR: Will you have a whisky?

JULIKA: It's terrible, gentlemen —

PROSECUTOR: What is?

JULIKA: Where's my handkerchief?

COUNSEL: You've been very much excited —

JULIKA: Where's my belt?

COUNSEL: Belt?

JULIKA: I had a belt before!

COUNSEL: Knobel, go and look for it.

JULIKA: Tortoise-shell. With a red buckle —

(The warder goes out, the prosecutor fills glasses)

Don't get the wrong idea, gentlemen —

PROSECUTOR: You need not tell us anything, Madame, unless you feel the urge to.

JULIKA: Thank you.

COUNSEL: Just tell us one thing, Mrs. Wadel. Is he your husband or isn't he?

JULIKA: I don't know —

COUNSEL: You don't know?

JULIKA: He is so different from the way I knew him — so . . .

COUNSEL: So cantankerous and stubborn, I know.

JULIKA: On the contrary.

PROSECUTOR: Drink the whisky, Madame. You really need not tell us anything.

JULIKA: On the contrary — he was so charming . . . It's terrible, gentlemen, this business with the belt!

COUNSEL: Calm yourself, Mrs. Wadel. I am firmly convinced that he is none other than your esteemed husband, otherwise we should never have exposed you to this threat, naturally.

JULIKA: He didn't threaten me. On the contrary . . .

PROSECUTOR: Why are you so excited?

JULIKA: I'm so happy.

PROSECUTOR: But?

JULIKA: He says his name is Rip van Winkle.

PROSECUTOR: His name is what?

JULIKA: Rip van Winkle . . . *(She suppresses the beginning of a sob)* Yes!

COUNSEL: Get a grip on yourself, Mrs. Wadel. You surely don't doubt that he's your husband!

JULIKA: I've never seen him like that — *(The sob breaks out)* He — was — so — charming —

(The cathedral clock begins to boom the hour; the booming and sobbing fade out together)

SCENE 12

Acoustics of a telephone.

SECRETARY: Yes, this is the Public Prosecutor's office. The Public Prosecutor asked me to ring you, Inspector. Unfortunately he is busy just now, and the matter is very urgent.

INSPECTOR: What's it about?

SECRETARY: The Public Prosecutor wishes to know whether there is or ever has been a person named Rip van Winkle. He feels he has heard the name before, but —

INSPECTOR: What was it again?

SECRETARY: Rip van Winkle.

INSPECTOR: Rip van Winkle — how do you spell it?

SECRETARY: Just as it's pronounced.

INSPECTOR: We'll look it up.

SECRETARY: The Public Prosecutor would be very grateful to you.

INSPECTOR: Not at all.

(The receiver is replaced)

SCENE 13

In the cell.

STRANGER: *(Is whistling)*

KNOBEL: You were right, Mr. van Winkle. The lady — yesterday — was mistaken. All that hunting around all day long was for nothing. Her belt was at home.

STRANGER: H'm.

KNOBEL: How's the hunger strike?

STRANGER: What's on the menu today?

KNOBEL: Barley soup, corn on the cob and stewed prunes.

STRANGER: No thanks.

(The warder picks up the pots and is about to carry the food on to other cells)

When am I going to get my whisky?

KNOBEL: I pass your request on to the legal gentlemen out in the office every day, but they say alcohol is forbidden to prisoners on remand — but who knows, Mr. van Winkle, perhaps you will be allowed into the town tomorrow.

STRANGER: I?

KNOBEL: Or the day after. Then you can drink as much whisky as you need.

STRANGER: What do you mean, into the town?

KNOBEL: I'm not supposed to talk about it, Mr. van Winkle.

STRANGER: What do you mean, into the town? Come on, out with it. What's this all about? Are they going to set me free — under a false name?

KNOBEL: Mr. van Winkle —

STRANGER: Come on, talk. What's going on here?

KNOBEL: Well —

STRANGER: Otherwise these stewed prunes won't leave my cell, Knobel, I'm warning you.

KNOBEL: It seems the lady took a great liking to you . . .

STRANGER: Go on.

KNOBEL: Anyhow, the lady went bail for you.

STRANGER: Bail?

KNOBEL: I happened to overhear it yesterday, a pretty big sum, if I heard right.

STRANGER: Bail? What for?

KNOBEL: Well — for you, Mr. van Winkle. The lady is in love with you, I noticed that the moment she came out of the cell . . . So that you can be given permission to go for a walk twice a week.

STRANGER: With her?

KNOBEL: Fresh air and so on, diversion, that can't do any harm, said the Public Prosecutor. And Mr. Dünner is also in favour of the idea.

He talked about the effect of seeing your country again; the lady is supposed to show you round our city.

STRANGER: H'm.

KNOBEL: We shall find out. In any case the request is being considered, otherwise they wouldn't have asked me: Do you think the prisoner is likely to behave obscenely in the street?

STRANGER: What did you say to that?

KNOBEL: I can't give any guarantee.

STRANGER: Good for you, Knobel.

KNOBEL: When someone has just come out of the jungle, I said, from Jamaica —

STRANGER: From Mexico.

KNOBEL: Mexico or Jamaica, it makes no difference, Mr. van Winkle; they don't believe in either.

STRANGER: *(Throws himself on the bed and laughs)* Go for walks!

(The warder picks up the last pot)

KNOBEL: Believe me, Mr. van Winkle, if I didn't have a family I wouldn't carry on for another day. I'd unlock the door, just to make those legal gentlemen open their eyes — I'd unlock the door with this key and the two of us could go straight off to the jungle!

VOICES: *(Shouts for the warder from outside)*

KNOBEL: All right, all right, I'm just coming.

STRANGER: Go for walks and admire their Botanical Garden, as though I hadn't seen all those plants in real life! Fancy feeding swans, with a view of the mountains — and forgetting that there are real volcanoes . . .

RIP VAN WINKLE

KNOBEL: You've seen real volcanoes?

STRANGER: Volcanoes, my dear Knobel, that's what I call a landscape, mountains with red-hot lava that stops you from sleeping, it lights up the night so —

KNOBEL: Well I'm damned.

STRANGER: And the earth shakes with the rumbling.

KNOBEL: Well I'm damned!

STRANGER: I was working on a plantation at the time. Suddenly the place reeked of sulphur. What's this? I thought. And when the ground got too hot under my feet, I naturally made off. An hour later, when I looked back, there was already a little hill. Next morning there was so much smoke you could scarcely see the sun, and it was thundering so loudly everyone left their huts; the church bells pealed day and night, and a mountain grew before our eyes; the birds wheeled this way and that, the clouds went red. And the dogs whined and crept into corners. On the sixth day it burst. Crack, and red-hot stones flew up into the air.

KNOBEL: A volcano?

STRANGER: What else?

KNOBEL: Well I'm damned.

STRANGER: And the way the lava pours out — I'll tell you about that another time, my dear Knobel, bring the stewed prunes now.

KNOBEL: Lava?

STRANGER: It spurts out like the blood from a black bull, it glows like a blast furnace, and then it comes closer, a red-hot mush as high as a house, slowly but inexorably; the forests disappear, there is a cracking and rumbling, prayer is no use, it comes slowly towards the village, creeps into the streets bringing red-hot death; the houses are drowned and only a church tower shows where the village used to be; afterwards everything is like slag, black and violet. And as silent as death, as silent as eternity.

KNOBEL: Well I'm damned.

STRANGER: Only the mountain goes on belching out smoke, the clouds are red — and anyone who has once experienced it, my good Knobel, knows how hot it is inside the earth and what it means to be a human being, a guest on this earth . . . Now bring the stewed prunes!

SCENE 14

Acoustics of a telephone.

PROSECUTOR: That's a joke, my dear fellow —

VOICE: That's all I can tell you.

PROSECUTOR: Thanks. A fairy story. And I've been making enquiries in all the government offices; of course they don't know who Rip van Winkle is — a fairy story!

VOICE: I can't remember where I read it, but it's the title of an American fairy story, I know that for sure, I can't remember any more than that —

PROSECUTOR: That's enough. Thanks a lot. You've done me a great service, seriously —

VOICE: See you this evening then.

PROSECUTOR: Regards to your wife —

(The prosecutor hangs up)

A fairy story! . . . Miss Schmidt, you needn't make any more calls. Take a fresh piece of paper and write.

(The secretary puts a sheet of paper in her typewriter. The sound of typing is heard in the background)

(Dictates) Rip van Winkle. An American fairy story. Rip van Winkle was an old Dutchman who had been living for many years in New

Amsterdam; everyone knew him as a good, hard-working man. One afternoon he walked along the Hudson and climbed the black cliffs of Manhattan to have a little nap. Suddenly, as he was sleeping in the sun, Rip heard a strange rumbling, hollow like underground thunder, that gave him no peace. He set out —

SECRETARY: Gave him no peace.

PROSECUTOR: He set out to investigate the strange rumbling, and entered a cave he had never seen before. In the cave a company of jolly gnomes were playing skittles, that was the rumbling noise, and when they recognized Rip, the good Dutchman, they left him no peace till he drank with them. In return Rip had to help them to set up the skittles. The drinking and skittling, the rumbling and laughter, went on and on; no sooner had poor Rip set up the heavy skittles than the gnomes laughed and knocked them all down again, with a cracking sound like thunder. — When Rip van Winkle finally woke up, he was still lying on the black cliffs of Manhattan, the sun was shining as though barely an hour had passed, but lo and behold —

SECRETARY: — as though barely an hour had passed.

PROSECUTOR: But lo and behold, when Rip van Winkle returned to his little town, everything was different; years had passed. His house was dilapidated, the garden overgrown with weeds, and Rip didn't recognize a single soul. But the people didn't know him either, only his name. So he stood there, a stranger in a strange town. —

SECRETARY: — only his name.

PROSECUTOR: So he stood there, a stranger in a strange town.

(The typing stops)

Good.

SECRETARY: Is that all, sir?

PROSECUTOR: Yes, that's all.

SCENE 15

In the café. Same noises as previously in the café.

JULIKA: Why are you so quiet?

(The espresso machine hisses)

I asked why you are so quiet.

STRANGER: I love you, Julika.

JULIKA: But?

STRANGER: I can't stand all these questions.

JULIKA: Anatol —

STRANGER: I'm not Anatol, I'm not your husband, Julika, and if you can't grasp that — maybe your husband used to put up with it, that's to say, until he couldn't stand it any longer.

JULIKA: What?

STRANGER: These questions, where have you been? . . . Waiter!

JULIKA: Please!

STRANGER: I've been in the jungle, my dear. More than that I'm not telling you, and if you don't want to believe me, then forget it, and if you can't forget it, then I shall go back to the jungle . . . Waiter!

JULIKA: Why are you so annoyed?

STRANGER: Waiter!

JULIKA: I thought a walk in the fresh air, a few hours of freedom, would do you good, I thought you would enjoy looking round the town. Don't you remember how often we used to sit in this alcove? With Stoll and all the others. They have always said, Anatol is dead. Only I knew that my husband would come back one day. Just imagine, they were already planning a memorial exhibition, an Anatol Wadel Memorial Exhibition. No, I said, my husband isn't dead —

WAITER: What would you like, sir?

STRANGER: Another whisky.

WAITER: Very good, sir.

JULIKA: You shouldn't drink so much.

STRANGER: I'm thirsty, my dear, and quite apart from that, I'm not going to let anyone prescribe how much I'm to drink. For the last time: I'm not your husband, Julika. Why won't you admit that? It's such a pity. You would be such a magnificent woman, full of life —

JULIKA: I feel better than I ever used to.

STRANGER: You see?

JULIKA: I really was mortally ill.

STRANGER: If you say so. But in that case, why do you keep wanting me to be your missing husband, who made you so ill, according to you, mortally ill? Why? I don't understand you, Julika.

JULIKA: I don't understand you either.

STRANGER: Is that a reason for thinking I'm your husband? As I said, you're an enchanting woman; I'm not saying that because of the bail which you put up for me, in your enthusiasm; seriously, I regret with all my heart, Julika, that we didn't meet earlier on in life. Believe me, the moment you stop thinking I'm your missing husband, you become beautiful and lively; I've met very few such women in my life —

WAITER: One whisky.

STRANGER: Thanks. — We could have such wonderful fun, Julika. If you could just stop talking about your missing husband all the time, about his studio, about his habits. What's all that to me?

JULIKA: Anatol —

STRANGER: I don't care how much you call me Anatol, I'm not Anatol.

JULIKA: And if I prove it to you?

STRANGER: Prove what?

JULIKA: That you're my husband.

STRANGER: Julika —

JULIKA: What is it?

STRANGER: I should have to murder you, Julika, as I murdered my first wife.

(The espresso machine hisses)

JULIKA: You can see for yourself that everyone recognizes you. That's Stoll who just nodded.

STRANGER: Who is Stoll?

JULIKA: Stoll, the writer!

STRANGER: He keeps gawping the whole time.

JULIKA: He can't believe his eyes, he can't believe you're back. Otherwise he would have come over long ago. Everyone recognizes you; as we came here through the streets everyone greeted you, even if you just stare into space. You're funny. Do you think I should have taken you up to my flat, if you weren't my husband? —

STRANGER: Waiter!

JULIKA: What do you take me for?

STRANGER: Waiter!

JULIKA: You have to be back in jail by six —

STRANGER: Waiter!

JULIKA: I'll go with you.

STRANGER: Another whisky.

WAITER: Certainly, sir.

STRANGER: And suppose I don't go back to jail?

JULIKA: What do you mean?

STRANGER: Suppose I beat it?

JULIKA: You won't do that, my dear.

STRANGER: Why not?

JULIKA: You won't do it for my sake.

STRANGER: How sure you are.

JULIKA: You know perfectly well — if you leave me in the lurch a second time —

STRANGER: Then you'll get T.B. again, I know, and I shall be your murderer.

(He bangs the table so that the glasses rattle)

JULIKA: What is it?

(Short pause. The waiter comes)

WAITER: A whisky?

STRANGER: I'd like my bill.

WAITER: One moment, sir.

STRANGER: I haven't much time.

WAITER: One moment.

(The waiter passes on; he can be heard at other tables)

JULIKA: Why are you looking at me like that?

STRANGER: I thought you loved me.

JULIKA: Don't I?

STRANGER: Instead of that, you have only one aim: to make sure I'm condemned to be your husband. It's ten to six, I know! There is one single person in this city who loves me, and that's my warder, who believes me when I tell him who I am. He doesn't imagine he knows me. But you, all of you, all you want is that I shall not dare to be myself — you too, my dear . . .

WAITER: You'd like your bill, sir?

STRANGER: Yes, please.

(The espresso machine hisses)

SCENE 16

In the studio of the ballet school. The same music and sounds as in scene three.

VOICE: Georges! Georges!

GEORGES: Qu'est-ce qu'il y a?

VOICE: Telephone.

GEORGES: Je travaille!

VOICE: C'est Julika.

GEORGES: M'excusez, Messieurs, dames. Je reviendrai tout de suite. Continuez votre exercice.

(Georges goes into the phone box so that — as in scene three — the music is heard only muted)

Hello? — Yes, speaking. How are you, Julika? You're in Paris? — No? — I see. — Why must you hear my voice? — So it is him. — I can't understand what you're saying when you cry, Julika. — It's a sacrifice, I understand, a sacrifice on your part, but you have to make it. — Not at all, Julika, you must do what makes you happy, even if it makes you happy to renounce and feel sorry for yourself. — That's just it. I said that's just why you're leaving me, Julika, you're a sufferer, you don't love him any more than you do me, you like it when a man has a bad conscience on your account, and I have no gift for that, as you know. — Yes, Julika, that's all I have to say to you. — Hello? Hello! — Hello? . . .

(He replaces the receiver, returns to the ballet studio)

Messieurs, dames, nous continuons.

SCENE 17

In the Public Prosecutor's office.

FERSTEL: That's all I can tell you, Mr. Public Prosecutor.

PROSECUTOR: Thank you, Mr. Ferstel. And as I said: don't be annoyed by the fact that the expression "hair oil gangster" keeps cropping up in the records. As you have seen, it is in quotation marks — it's an expression used by our prisoner.

FERSTEL: I shall sue him for slander.

PROSECUTOR: Just one more question, Mr. Ferstel.

FERSTEL: Go ahead.

PROSECUTOR: Have you any connection with Jamaica?

FERSTEL: Why? What do you mean?

PROSECUTOR: I am not enquiring into your business contacts, Mr. Ferstel; I merely want to know whether you talked to Anatol Wadel about Jamaica while he was working on your portrait bust?

FERSTEL: It's possible.

PROSECUTOR: Aha.

FERSTEL: I have a house in Jamaica.

PROSECUTOR: Aha.

FERSTEL: Why?

(The Prosecutor rises; so does Ferstel)

PROSECUTOR: Thank you, Mr. Ferstel. We are very relieved — if I may say so — that you have not been murdered.

FERSTEL: Murdered?

PROSECUTOR: You see, our prisoner absolutely insists that he murdered you years ago.

FERSTEL: Me?

PROSECUTOR: In Jamaica — yes.

FERSTEL: Would you believe it!

(The Prosecutor has accompanied Ferstel to the door; a brief goodbye is heard, then the door shuts)

COUNSEL: There you are!

PROSECUTOR: You feel relieved, Counsellor.

COUNSEL: Don't you?

(The Prosecutor lights a cigar)

Thank you, I don't smoke cigars.

PROSECUTOR: So that's the hair oil gangster . . .

COUNSEL: Our prisoner has never murdered anyone; I said so from the start; it was all a lot of twaddle.

PROSECUTOR: That's true . . .

COUNSEL: But?

PROSECUTOR: I'm gradually beginning to understand what it's all about. Anatol Wadel was a man like so many others, a man who demanded too much of himself. With the result that he didn't live, he acted a part which he felt he owed to himself. Hence he had a bad conscience, a life-long sense of being in debt; everyone feels like that who doesn't accept himself. Instead of throwing that hair oil gangster downstairs when he refused to pay — no, he felt he had to be a mature and superior man, he smiled with maturity and superiority, but in exchange he murdered the man in his dreams. You see, we all know so well what we ought to be like, till the time comes when we no longer know who we are. That's to say, till we're simply not real any more. Because we don't accept our own reality. Everything becomes a phantasm — that's the story of Rip van Winkle, it seems to me.

COUNSEL: How do you mean?

PROSECUTOR: Those ridiculous skittles that Rip van Winkle had to set up, so that the gnomes could knock them down over and over again, what are they, Counsellor, but the ludicrously excessive demands we make upon ourselves? A task that is quite impossible to carry out, a senseless drudgery, but he wastes his whole life trying to carry it out till suddenly he wakes up, that is to say, he accepts himself. But what happens then? He goes back to his home town and finds that his real position in this world is quite different from what he and the others would like it to be. And the man who has woken up is a stranger in a strange city, an unknown man, a man without a name . . . Only we can't tolerate a man without a name, the man who has woken up is forced back into his old part, the unreal part he has outgrown.

(A knock at the door)

I simply ask myself, Counsellor, what is going to come of all this. I don't feel in the least relieved.

(A knock at the door)

Come in.

KNOBEL: The car is here, sir.

PROSECUTOR: Thank you. So we're going to Anatol Wadel's studio. Perhaps you will go on ahead with the lady, Counsellor. We'll follow with the prisoner a bit later.

COUNSEL: Very well, Public Prosecutor.

PROSECUTOR: We shall see what comes of it.

SCENE 18

In the studio. The nearby cathedral clock is booming.

COUNSEL: So this is his studio?

JULIKA: Can you understand now, Counsellor, why he curses the cathedral so? It's not so bad when it's just the clock striking — but the eleven o'clock chimes! You'll hear them in a quarter of an hour.

COUNSEL: They should be here at any moment.

JULIKA: Look, these are the last pieces of work he did.

COUNSEL: Ah.

JULIKA: They're all dried up. Unfortunately. I didn't touch anything, you know. I look upon his art as sacred, all art in fact —

COUNSEL: What are those things?

JULIKA: Rough drafts. There's no point in looking at them as they are now; they're all wrapped up still. To stop the clay from drying. But of course it has dried up just the same by now. Five years is a long time. Why are you looking at me like that?

COUNSEL: If I may say so, Mrs. Wadel — they look like mummies.

JULIKA: Yes, yes, of course, with this sacking round them.

COUNSEL: They do, don't they?

JULIKA: If you touch them, they will all crumble away, I'm afraid . . . I hope I'm doing the right thing in being present at this confrontation.

COUNSEL: Definitely.

JULIKA: Have you a cigarette, Counsellor?

COUNSEL: Oh, certainly.

JULIKA: What a happy time it was when he worked here. Although he made me ill — thanks. — It's the finest studio in the whole town: with this view over the roofs, with the cooing pigeons outside the window, and on a clear day you can actually see the mountains. I can't understand why he won't come back to this studio. I can't understand it.

COUNSEL: Did he sleep here too?

JULIKA: How do you mean?

COUNSEL: Did he live here, sleep, cook — work?

JULIKA: And how he worked! Look, this is a bronze. His last. It's in the National Museum.

COUNSEL: Is that you?

JULIKA: No.

COUNSEL: Sorry.

JULIKA: But just look — how abstract it is.

COUNSEL: Yes, very.

JULIKA: Here — this is a portrait of me.

COUNSEL: Ah.

JULIKA: What do you think of it?

COUNSEL: It's also — very abstract . . .

JULIKA: Isn't it?

COUNSEL: And then this view over the city! Forgive me, but I simply can't get over this view. You can even see the river. I can't understand any more than you can, Mrs. Wadel, how a man can prefer to live in prison rather than in this magnificent studio —

(The doorbell rings)

JULIKA: My God!

COUNSEL: Keep calm, Mrs. Wadel.

JULIKA: He's coming.

COUNSEL: As I said: don't contradict him when he denies things; we'll just give him time; chat about anything that comes into your head, we'll pretend we're here quite by chance; meanwhile he's bound to notice these sculptures.

JULIKA: And if he smashes them up?

COUNSEL: That will be an admission that he is their creator.

(The doorbell rings again)

JULIKA: No — you open the door, Counsellor.

(The Counsel goes to the door and opens it)

VOICE: *(On the landing)* Any old rags and bones? . . . Any old rags and bones? . . .

(The door is shut again)

JULIKA: What were we talking about?

COUNSEL: The hearing takes place tomorrow, and there is no doubt that the court will find that he is your husband — only, as I have said, it would be so much better if he would admit it voluntarily.

JULIKA: Certainly.

COUNSEL: It's his last chance. What's that?

JULIKA: A portrait.

COUNSEL: Of a criminal?

JULIKA: Don't you recognize it?

COUNSEL: Ferstel?

JULIKA: A weak piece of work, in my opinion, far too naturalistic. That's the man he "murdered." And yet you should have seen how Anatol behaved in reality towards this millionaire when he refused to pay him! Not a single loud word, not a trace of anger; Anatol simply renounced the money. I have never known anyone less capable of arguing than Anatol. He is much too refined for that, you see. If something goes wrong, he always considers it his fault. That's why I love him so.

(A knock at the door)

Come in.

COUNSEL: Come in!

(The door opens)

JULIKA: Good morning, Mr. Public Prosecutor.

PROSECUTOR: Good morning, Mrs. Wadel.

JULIKA: Where's my husband?

PROSECUTOR: Knobel?

KNOBEL: Yes, sir?

PROSECUTOR: Bring the gentleman in.

(Knobel brings in the stranger)

JULIKA: Anatol!

STRANGER: What's all this?

PROSECUTOR: This is Anatol Wadel's studio.

STRANGER: So what?

PROSECUTOR: Won't you take off your coat, Mr. van Winkle? I'm sure there's a hook somewhere.

STRANGER: What the hell did you bring me here for?

JULIKA: Anatol!

STRANGER: What do you want from me? . . . I'm not going to take my coat off.

COUNSEL: There's actually a coat-hanger here.

STRANGER: What do you want from me? I asked . . . Don't touch me, Mr. Dünner; that's something I can't stand; if you do, I shall slap your face.

(The stranger throws away the coat-hanger)

For the last time: what do you want from me?

JULIKA: Don't you know where you are?

STRANGER: I've had enough of this. I've told you the truth: I'm having an affair with this lady —

JULIKA: Anatol!

STRANGER: But what did you bring me to this dusty old studio for? I ask you. What for? It makes me sick, all this junk. What has it got to do with life? What has it got to do with me? Nothing but mummies . . . a head like this, for example.

JULIKA: That's you yourself.

STRANGER: It should be destroyed.

COUNSEL: As I said, I know nothing about art —

STRANGER: Nor do I.

COUNSEL: But I believe your criticism is too harsh. I've read that every artist has moods in which he doesn't approve of his own work, in which he can't understand it.

STRANGER: I'm not an artist.

COUNSEL: All the same —

STRANGER: And I suppose this is meant to be Ferstel?

JULIKA: Don't think about Ferstel now.

STRANGER: I enjoy thinking about him. I murdered him — whereas your husband condescended to make a bust of that gangster, quite apart from the fact that it's a lousy cast!

COUNSEL: Only an expert could see that, Mr. Wadel —

STRANGER: My name isn't Wadel!! *(He has yelled the last bit; he continues with an ominous calm)* If I hear that name once more — I shall smash all this rubbish in pieces.

JULIKA: Don't you recognize that it's your own work?

STRANGER: I recognize an unparalleled conspiracy. I love this lady, admittedly, and why should I deny it? She was brought into my cell; we were allowed out together; what has happened has happened, and I admit frankly: I love this lady. Isn't that enough? Don't imagine that just because of that I'm going to be coerced into acting the part of the lady's husband.

JULIKA: Anatol!

STRANGER: I'm not her husband.

JULIKA: Heavens above —

STRANGER: Either you love me as I am and do without your Anatol — or . . .

COUNSEL: Or?

STRANGER: Or devil take him and everything that reminds me of him, everything — everything — everything —

(The Stranger is heard throwing a piece of sculpture on the floor)

JULIKA: *(Screams)*

(One thud follows another)

COUNSEL: *(Cries out)* Mr. Wadel!

STRANGER: I'm not Wadel — I'm not Wadel . . .

(The thuds are drowned by the eleven o'clock chimes)

SCENE 19

The chimes die away. We are in court. There is a slight rustling of paper, then silence.

PROSECUTOR: Sentence will now be pronounced. — The accused, who three weeks ago crossed our frontier and was thereafter guilty of assault and battery against a customs official engaged in the execution of his duty, and who while in custody gave his name as Rip van Winkle without being able to produce any documentary evidence in support of his claim to this name, has done nothing to disprove the suspicion that he is the missing Anatol Wadel, and on the grounds of the aforesaid evidence, and in spite of his refusal to confess, he is condemned by this court as from today once more to bear the name Anatol Wadel.

In recognition of his services to the city (as Anatol Wadel) the court will refrain from imposing upon the accused the costs of the case, and since the Academy of Art has declared its willingness to pay the fine for the aforesaid assault and battery and to meet any other outstanding debts to which the missing man is liable, and since there is absolutely no evidence to support the prisoner's assertion that he has committed murders, the court has further decided to release Mr. Anatol Wadel from custody as from today.

JULIKA: Anatol!

PROSECUTOR: I declare the Court adjourned.

(The sound of voices and people rising from their seats)

COUNSEL: Congratulations, Mr. Wadel, congratulations. Didn't you hear? You're to be released.

JULIKA: I'll call a taxi —

COUNSEL: Why don't you say anything?

JULIKA: The Press people are already waiting outside, but don't worry, my dear, we shall be quite alone in your studio.

(Julika and the Stranger move away amidst the sound of voices, while the Counsel remains behind)

COUNSEL: And he goes off without even shaking hands with me! A client who is discharged and not a word of thanks — such a thing has never happened to me before.

PROSECUTOR: You feel hurt, Dünner?

COUNSEL: I certainly do.

PROSECUTOR: What is he supposed to thank you for?

COUNSEL: Well, I mean —

PROSECUTOR: I can understand his feelings.

COUNSEL: He's free. What more can anyone want, Public Prosecutor, I ask you? Free, and he treats me, his defence counsel, as though I didn't exist; you saw for yourself, as though I didn't exist.

PROSECUTOR: Don't get so excited about it.

COUNSEL: Didn't I do my best?

PROSECUTOR: It's a hard verdict for him.

COUNSEL: What do you mean?

(The Prosecutor opens a door)

PROSECUTOR: After you, my dear Dünner, after you.

(They enter. The door is closed)

COUNSEL: What do you mean by a hard verdict?

PROSECUTOR: I should have liked to have spared him that . . . Let's have a whisky . . . We have condemned a man to be what he used to be.

COUNSEL: I don't understand.

PROSECUTOR: Unfortunately we're doing it all the time.

COUNSEL: We make ourselves an image of someone and don't let him escape from this image. We know that he used to be so and so, and it doesn't matter what has happened to him, we can't tolerate him changing. You can see for yourself, even his wife can't put up with it; she wants him to be the way he was, and she calls that love.

COUNSEL: But really, Public Prosecutor —

PROSECUTOR: We're not prepared for the nameless, for the living, we can't rest until we have condemned it to a name that no longer applies to it. —

(He can be heard filling the glasses)

PUBLIC PROSECUTOR: Read the legend of Rip van Winkle some time. I can't explain it any better than that. A person wakes up to himself, but we —

(A knock at the door)

PROSECUTOR: Come in.

(The warder enters)

PROSECUTOR: What's the matter, Knobel? You're as white as a sheet.

KNOBEL: Mr. Public Prosecutor —

PROSECUTOR: Out with it, man!

KNOBEL: They say he has strangled her —

COUNSEL: Strangled?

PROSECUTOR: His wife?

KNOBEL: No sooner was he outside, they say —

PROSECUTOR: Is she dead?

KNOBEL: No, Public Prosecutor, but almost — they say —

(Brief silence)

PROSECUTOR: So where is he?

KNOBEL: Back in his cell.

PROSECUTOR: Good. Thank you, Knobel, thanks.

COUNSEL: What about his wife?

KNOBEL: The ambulance should be here at any moment.

(The warder leaves)

PROSECUTOR: Sit down, Counsellor, and drink your whisky.

COUNSEL: God in heaven . . .

PROSECUTOR: This time I shall defend him.